D0117137

RELATIONAL
LEADERSHIP

Leading as Jesus Led

David Ferguson
in cooperation with
The Center for Biblical Leadership

Relationship Press

Relationship Press • P.O. Box 201808 • Austin, TX 78720-1808
Phone: 1-800-881-8008 • Fax: 1-512-795-0853

ISBN–1-893307-36-0

Table of Contents

Acknowledgements

It might seem, at first thought, unnecessary to address the subject of leadership from a "relational" perspective. As you embark on this study, however, you will find that leadership is fundamentally about intimate relationships: first with the One who has called us, and secondly with those we serve. With this background, it should not be surprising that the development of this Relational Leadership resource involved a diverse team that needs to be gratefully acknowledged for their significant contributions.

Several individuals contributed to my own leadership journey over the decades, including my father, Roy, whose military background contributed to my understanding of the need to focus on objectives so that my life would not inevitably wander, and my grandfather, Jerry, who modeled quiet, gentle servanthood. In my professional and ministry undertakings, Gordon Carlson trusted me with leadership at a young age, and Pastor Roger Barrier of Casas Adobes Church in Tucson, Arizona has for the past decade shaped my appreciation for a leader's humility and teachable heart, lived out in interdependent fellowship. Dr. Thomas Parker at Trinity Bible College and Theological Seminary shared lectures on management and leadership which years ago served to challenge my initial academic work on leadership principles from the life of Christ. Emmett McCoy modeled essential leadership traits for me in the corporate world, including integrity, loyalty, and dependability—traits that provide an ethical foundation from which to lead.

The "laboratory" for these relational leadership principles has been the gifted Intimate Life Ministries team with whom God allows me to serve. Without the calling, passion, energy, and support of each of them, these principles would remain untested, lacking credibility and relevance. Of particular support in this "laboratory" have been Dr. Lewis Alexander and the team he leads through the Center for Relational Leadership (CRL). In both ministry and corporate settings the CRL team routinely sees the reality of these principles lived out in the lives of those they serve. Critical to this relational leadership "laboratory" has been the CRL work in the corporate sector with McCoy's Building Supply. Without the continued vision, encouragement, and support of Brian McCoy, Chuck Churchwell, and the entire McCoy's Executive Team, the continued refinement and development of this work would not have been possible.

Next have been the combined contributions of several of the Great Commandment Network Strategic Partners who have helped to bring this resource collection together. Larry Duncan and the Center for Biblical Leadership (CBL) team at the Church of God of Prophecy international offices contributed the vision, resources, and editorial and publishing support to make this revised edition and leader's guide possible.

CBL work in California, Florida, Nigeria, and the Bahamas provided essential field-testing opportunities, as did similar support from Leonard Albert and Ray Hughes, who lead lay ministries with the Church of God (Cleveland, TN). Dr. Dennis Lindsay and Dr. Jack Hatcher with Christ for the Nations in Dallas supported the initial release and video product development with a critical international audience of Bible college directors and students from around the world. The creative talents of Mike Frazier and a partnership with the Southern Baptist Radio and Television Commission in Fort Worth provided the supportive media product.

Finally, and with deep gratitude, Terri Snead's creative development of the relational leadership message makes each chapter come alive, while Jim Walter's structural support and leader's material allow instructors to facilitate the course with confidence. John Duncan provided invaluable editorial support, while the White Wing Publishing staff, including Lonzo Kirkland, Joann Nope, Diann Stewart, David Smith, Virginia Chatham, and Elizabeth Witt, provided proof-reading, a creative cover design, and an easy-to-follow layout, all of which resulted in a user-friendly product.

May each of us "decrease that He might increase" as we experience together the blessings of leading as Jesus led.

David

Preface

"Not so among you." With these few words, the saddened heart of the Savior pleaded for a uniqueness in the way His people approach the issue of leadership (Luke 22:26 KJV). His words were occasioned by the disciples' self-focused embrace of worldly ways.

In a day when self-focus has become so commonplace in church and ministry, is it possible that we might encounter the Spirit's reminder: "It is not about you, it is about Me!" Such is our hope.

In a day when His people seem so preoccupied with worldly considerations - what we have acquired, accomplished, or achieved - is it possible that we might be arrested by the Savior's prayerful plea: "May they be not of the world, even as I am not of the world." Such is our hope.

As you embark on this study in *Relational Leadership*, we encourage you to pause and listen to the Lord. See if you do not hear in your heart these same whispered words . . . "not so among you." If there is not something distinctive about how His people lead, then perhaps we have missed His heart.

We are honored and humbled to share in this journey as we explore together the privilege and responsibility of "leading as Jesus led."

Dr. David Ferguson
and the Intimate Life Staff

Welcome to *Relational Leadership!*

Relational Leadership is a course of study designed to equip you and your ministry team to meet the enormous challenges of leadership in the 21st century.

This *Relational Leadership* workbook is intended to serve as the participants' guide for the course. It includes everything participants need to thoroughly experience the *Relational Leadership* resource.

This workbook includes the following features:

• **Key Relational Leadership Principles**—These are introduced through the text of the workbook. They appear as text boxes in each chapter. Leadership principles are then discussed in the text of the workbook.

• **Personal Exercises**—These exercises are designed for individuals working through this resource with a fellow leader or as a participant in a class setting. The goal is to provide the opportunity to process the content, come to interact with one or two others, and experience the appropriate relational principle.

• **Experiencing the Word Together**—Each chapter will include at least one opportunity to truly experience God's Word together. At these times, participants will have the opportunity to become "doers of the Word" (James 1:22).

• **My Team Journal**—Leaders are given the opportunity to take notes and keep journal entries as their team shares responses to workbook exercises. Small group participants may also want to use this section to record responses of fellow group members. These notes will serve as reminders of the unique needs of each individual.

• **Session Outline**—Each chapter contains a structured outline that summarizes the chapter contents, including the personal exercises. These may be used as participant worksheets or as a guide for the instructor.

• **Additional Resources**—Each chapter includes a list of works referenced in the text, along with additional materials which may prove helpful to the participants as they continue their growth in relational leadership.

Participants should note that the *Relational Leadership* course can be experienced . . .

• individually, as a self study.

- with a partner.
- with a class or small group.
- with your ministry team.

Relational Leadership sessions can also be formatted for use . . .

- as a weekly "stand-alone" course.
- as curriculum for a weekend retreat.
- as a "continuing education" component of regular
  leadership team meetings.
- as leadership training for prospective leaders.

How to Get the Most Out of This Resource

In order to get the most benefit and blessing from this resource, we urge you to do the following:

1. **Set aside time each week to read the chapter and work through the Personal Exercises.** This will prepare you for your interactions with a partner or small group and enrich your personal understanding of each chapter.

2. **If you are working through this resource with a friend or fellow leader, we urge you to make time each week to work through and discuss the exercises.** Make your meetings a priority in your schedule and come prepared to interact appropriately.

3. **If you are working through this resource with a small group, we urge you to make it a priority to attend each small group session.** Make your meetings a consistent part of your schedule and come prepared to interact appropriately. You may also want to make notes and then reflect on the responses of fellow group members from each meeting. We urge you to get to know each person in your group in a meaningful way, show interest in their lives, and demonstrate supportive care.

4. **The following "Participant Promise" page presents some ways in which you can make the most of your experience with this workbook.** We suggest that you read it over and carefully discuss it with your partner or group before making this commitment.

Participant Promise

We invite each participant to commit to the following in order to enhance their personal and communal experience of this resource:

1. I will spend time between sessions completing the chapters with honesty and sincerity.

2. I will refrain from criticizing other leaders; instead, I will be open and willing for God to show me how I can better lead those He has entrusted to my care.

3. I will participate in learning sessions fully, openly, and honestly.

4. I will seek to give care as others may need it and receive care as I may need it.

5. I will be willing to receive feedback from those who know me in my group, team, or family so that I might experience the growth God intends for me through this course.

_____

Name   Date

Chapter 1

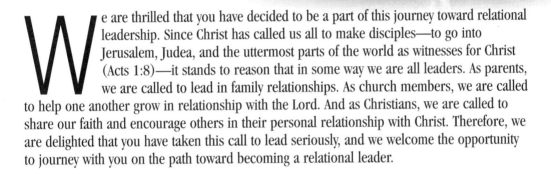

The Critical Need for Relational Leadership

We are thrilled that you have decided to be a part of this journey toward relational leadership. Since Christ has called us all to make disciples—to go into Jerusalem, Judea, and the uttermost parts of the world as witnesses for Christ (Acts 1:8)—it stands to reason that in some way we are all leaders. As parents, we are called to lead in family relationships. As church members, we are called to help one another grow in relationship with the Lord. And as Christians, we are called to share our faith and encourage others in their personal relationship with Christ. Therefore, we are delighted that you have taken this call to lead seriously, and we welcome the opportunity to journey with you on the path toward becoming a relational leader.

Before we begin this journey, though, we want to recommend that you find another person or group to go through this course with you. As the name implies, this course is about relationships. Therefore, it will be essential that you have at least one other friend or partner in ministry to experience this course with you. This will enable you to discuss and experience these principles in a relationship. In other words, it will not serve you well to try to experience a "relational" course alone.

Ideally, we hope that you will choose to go through this course with a group—either with a group that you lead, a group of fellow leaders, or even a group of potential leaders. We have found that this provides the ideal environment for the Lord to do the most work in our lives. With that said, let's get started!

First, take a moment to reflect on the topic of leadership as a whole. Use the following questions to help focus your attention and begin your study.

- As you think about the subject of leadership, what comes to your mind? What do you associate with leadership as it is typically portrayed or practiced?

- How would you describe your own concept of effective Christian leadership?

- What do you sense may be needed in Christian leadership today?

In this course, we will define an approach to leadership that we will call "Relational Leadership." We will then see how that approach may provide the answers to some of the most significant crises the church faces today.

WHY DO WE NEED A DIFFERENT TYPE OF LEADERSHIP?

Imagine a world where immorality is rampant and corruption is widespread. Imagine a society in which truth is mocked as if it does not exist. Imagine a culture in which materialism has become a god and the persecution of Christians has become commonplace. Can you picture a world in which these things are not only a reality, but the norm? If you responded, "That describes our world now. That description fits our culture today," you would be correct.

Indeed, it's true. Our 21st century world is filled with all of the negatives and unpleasantness that we've described. Yet an examination of history reveals that those same descriptors also applied to the world in which the 1st century church operated. The early Christians encountered the same challenges of immorality, materialism, corruption, persecution, and skepticism that confront us today.

The irony is that the 1st century church turned the world upside down for Jesus Christ in the face of these obstacles that have brought the 21st century church to its knees. How is it that they set the world on fire with the Gospel, and yet, at times, we seem to barely survive?

A Crisis of Identity in the 21st Century Church

We must ask ourselves, "What did the 1st century Christians have that made such a difference?" After all, the 21st century church is much better equipped than its 1st century counterpart in many ways. We have capable and professional leaders, gifted communicators who are well-educated and armed with the latest ministry techniques and methodologies. We have a wealth of creative materials and tools to assist us in sharing the Gospel. We possess tremendous material blessings in the form of money and facilities. We have access to technologically advanced means of communication that allow us to beam the message of Christ around the globe. But despite all the resources we have at our disposal, the Western world is less open and receptive to Christianity than ever before.

[NOTE: It is important to recognize that the conditions we have been describing are chiefly symptomatic of Western societies. Churches in other parts of the world are facing their own unique challenges. In Africa, for instance, Christianity has experienced such phenomenal growth that there is a pressing need for an increase in the number of church leaders, as well as the establishment of effective processes by which to train them (Snook, 1992). As we tackle the issues affecting the church within our own societal context, we must remain aware of the varied challenges confronting Christians throughout the world.]

The Identity of the Early Church One key ingredient the early Christians possessed that the contemporary Western church seems to be missing is a clear sense of identity. The 1st century church had an identity as a people of love. You could not have looked into the early Christian community without finding people who were committed to a deep and profound Spirit-led intimacy with the God who is love. Furthermore, those early believers expressed that same love for one another as they gathered in fellowship. They took seriously the words of Jesus: "By this all men will know that you are my disciples, if you love one another" (John 13:35). The 1st century church embodied this imperative as they partnered together, freely shared their material goods, and actively lived out *agape* love.

This commitment to love was unmistakably the central aspect of the church's identity. Had their contemporaries asked, "Who are those Christians?" the reply would most likely have been, "Oh, they are the people who have a deep, loving relationship with Jesus, who claimed to be the Messiah. They are the people who have a deep, loving relationship with one another. They are the people who know how to love."

Indeed, several surviving works from the first few centuries of the Church's existence convey these very themes in their descriptions of the early Christians. In his *Apologeticus* of AD 197, Tertullian exclaimed, "See how these Christians love one another." The anonymous author of the 2nd century *Epistle to Diognetus* remarked of the early Christians, "They love all men . . . They are poor, yet make many rich . . . What the soul is in the body, that are Christians in the world." Such descriptions reflect the fact that the 1st century Christians placed great priority on those things that Jesus deemed most central to the faith. When the Pharisees asked Jesus what was the greatest commandment in the Scriptures, He responded by choosing one verse from Deuteronomy and one from Leviticus and explaining their importance to those who awaited His answer: "Love the Lord your God with all of your heart and mind and with all your soul and with all your strength. This is the first and greatest commandment. And the second commandment is like it:

Love your neighbor as yourself" (Matthew 22:37–39). The 1st century church lived out the Great Commandment as they demonstrated their love for God and for one another.

In contrast, how do you think the average person of our day would answer the question, "Who are those Christians?" They would probably say, "Oh, those are the people who don't believe in. . . . That's the group who insists on believing in. . . . Oh, yes, Christians are the ones who protest against. . . ."

Are the things we as Christians believe in, insist on, or protest against unimportant? Certainly not—at least not all of them. But as significant as those things may be, they must not become our sole identity. The 1st century church had a clear identity—an identity of love. That is what is often missing in our churches today. We must be a people who know how to love God and love others. When we lack this identity of love, we present a distorted view of faith, worship, and God, and we hinder our world from coming to know Christ.

> **Relational leadership is needed to help restore an identity of love to the 21st century church.**

Personal Exercise #1

We have described the early church as those who "turned the world upside down for Christ." Take special note of the following characteristics of the 1st century church, as it is described in the Book of Acts:

- They devoted themselves to the apostles' teaching, to fellowship, to the breaking of bread, and to prayer (Acts 2:42).
- They had a reputation of unity (v. 44).
- They generously shared personal goods with those in need (v. 45).
- Others took note that they had been with Jesus (4:13).
- They spoke the Word of the Lord with boldness (v. 31).
- They were of one heart and mind (v. 32).
- With great power, they gave witness, and abundant grace was upon them (v. 33).
- The people held them in high esteem (5:13).
- Multitudes of men and women were constantly added to their number (v. 14).
- They rejoiced that they had been considered worthy to suffer shame in His name (v. 41).

Take a moment and look over this list of characteristics again. Then finish the following sentence:

I would like to see more of the 1st century church expressed in the 21st century church. I would most like to see more . . . because. . . .

(For example: *I would most like to see more unity because disagreements in the church can be so harmful.*)

As directed by your facilitator, share your responses with one or two other participants, or with the entire group. You may want to record these responses in the Team Journal at the end of the chapter.

The Need for Restored Identity After examining the life of the early Christian community, it quickly becomes apparent that what the 21st century church needs most is not a *new* identity, but a *restoration* of our identity as a people of love. Could we not benefit greatly from more fully knowing how to love God and love others?

Imagine God looking down on our world where love has grown cold. Imagine Him saying, "Church, I have revealed Myself to you in My Word. I have given you the 66 books of the Bible that tell you what I want you to know. These books contain thousands of verses that give you wisdom and guidance for your life. Out of all these 66 books, do you think that you could live just four or five verses?" If God said that, which verses do you think He might want us to live out?

Undoubtedly, He would remind us of Christ's answer to the Pharisees and His charge to the disciples: "I want you to be a people who experience and express the Great Commandment heart of love, and then go forward to fulfill the Great Commission—making disciples of all the nations" (see Matthew 22:37–40; 28:19, 20).

Consider Christ's words to the disciples in the Upper Room. Jesus was about to die and depart from His friends, the leaders of His church. His final instructions included a very simple commandment. John 13:34, 35 tells us what was on Christ's heart as He prepared His leaders: "A new command I give to you: Love one another. As I have loved you, so you must love one another. By this all men will know that you are my disciples, if you love one another."

In Christ's charge to the disciples, we find three things. First, He gave them a purpose: "Love one another." Second, He affirmed the basis of their identity, thus sustaining their life purpose: "You are ones who have been loved." Finally, Christ offered up His vision for them: "The world will know you are My disciples because of your love for one another." Jesus' strategy was clear and revolutionary—as we come to experience Christ's love for us, we will be challenged with the call to love one another, and that testimony of love will draw others to Him.

The principle seems so simple, so obvious. "Love one another, as I have loved you." Yet this brief commandment is the key to relevance and effectiveness for the 21st century church. We believe that the Western church has experienced the residual blessings that go along with centuries of strong Christian beliefs and influences. However, many who became believers in recent years have had no one to teach them how to live out the relational aspects of the Gospel.

Effective discipleship that equips believers to truly love God and love others has been scarce. Therefore, the Western church has spent decades focusing on believing the "right" doctrines and behaving in the "right" ways. It is this narrow focus on belief and behavior, apart from authentic relationship, that has contributed to the irrelevance, dysfunction, and decline of the church in the Western world. Reversing these trends will require the 21st church to rediscover its relational roots. Similarly, the challenge for the rest of the world will be to avoid the mistakes of Western Christianity and, instead, fully embrace the identity that Christ declared in the Upper Room. All of us are people who are loved. Western and non-Western churches alike must embark on the journey of loving one another and expressing that love to a world without Christ so that they may be led to relationship with Him.

It is certainly not difficult to see that we are living in a world that needs to hear our testimony of a Savior who loves them. Neighbors are doing heartless things to neighbors. Nations are inflicting horrific destruction on other nations. Parents are cruel to children. Children are hurtful to parents and to one another. Doesn't it make sense that our God would want to send into this broken world a group of people, His church, which truly knows how to love?

The hard truth we must face is that the Western church has lost its identity; and as a result, our ministry lacks relevance and significance. Despite our best efforts and tireless exertion, we have little meaningful impact on the world around us. In order to change the church of today and increase the degree to which it can influence society in positive ways, we must have changed leaders.

Crises Among Those Who Lead

Just as the church is experiencing a crisis in its identity, church leaders also frequently face crises. We see evidence of this when we look at the "leadership vacuum"—the lack of qualified leaders to fill the God-anointed role of leading His people to become what He wants them to be. In some developing countries, people are coming to Christ at such a rapid pace that churches cannot keep up with the need for leaders to shepherd and disciple these new flocks.

We also see signs of a leadership crisis as we witness the moral and ethical failures that seem to grip so many leaders today. These failures are destroying our witness to a dying world and undermining the faith of the people of God. The growing divorce rate of leadership marriages and the failure of many leaders to pass faith on to their children provide evidence of the devastating toll that ministry can take on the family. There is also an alarmingly high rate of burnout among Christian leaders, many of whom report being ill-prepared to fulfill their call to ministry. Finally, and perhaps most tragically, many ministers admit that they have few close friends with whom they can safely share their struggles (Fuller Institute, 1991). Largely as a result of these varied crises in the lives of Christian leaders, the average tenure of pastors in Protestant churches has declined to just four years (Barna, 1998).

Personal Exercise #2

Think about a time when your own Christian growth was painfully impacted by ill-prepared, morally or ethically compromised, or burned-out leaders. When might you have been hurt, disappointed, or saddened by someone in Christian leadership?

Share your responses with your partner or small group. Make this an opportunity to express care for one another, not an opportunity for complaint or criticism. Leave out names or details that would identify a specific leader. Expressions of care might sound like:

I really regret that happened.

It makes me sad to hear about. . . .

I am very sorry. I know it must have hurt when. . . .

As directed by your facilitator, either share your responses with one or two participants or with the whole group. Be certain to give care to one another as each person shares. Your caring words might sound like the examples above. You may want to record these responses in the Team Journal at the end of the chapter.

Crises in Our Approaches to Leadership

Not only are there signs of crisis in the lives of church leaders, there is also evidence of crisis in our fundamental approaches to leadership. Even when our leaders manage to avoid the pitfalls of moral failure, family dysfunction, and burnout, there is often a great chasm between the leadership principles that they implement and what God desires. There are a variety of secular approaches to leadership that have found their way into the 21st century church. Here are a few examples you may recognize:

Chief Executive Officer. In this approach, one person, or a group of persons, tells everyone else what to do. There is no doubt that the church can sometimes benefit from a decisive leader who can take charge in critical moments. However, we must be careful not to endorse a domineering leadership style that can obscure the passion that God has for His people and become a hindrance to the fulfillment of the Great Commission.

Classic Management. This leadership style endorses using people and resources in order to accomplish tasks. Its motto is, "Get things done through people." Dr. John Kotter of the Harvard School of Business has made reference to the fact that most businesses in the Western world are over-managed and under-led (Kotter, 1996), and, unfortunately, this is true of many churches as well. One of the painful things about this approach is that people end up feeling used. People will respond to a great vision, but they will typically resist being used.

Management by Committee. In this approach, leaders seek to gain the approval of a majority of the people and equate that approval with the will of God.

Do What Everyone Else Is Doing. In this approach, leaders clearly identify a problem within their group, find someone else who has solved a similar problem, and then work hard to sell the people on someone else's solution. Often the leaders must expend enormous energy to overcome the people's resistance.

If we are not careful, we will introduce these worldly principles into the body of Christ and quench the moving of the Holy Spirit among His people.

Personal Exercise #3

Have you been painfully impacted by one of these approaches to leadership?

Share your responses with your partner or small group. Again, make this an opportunity to express care for one another, not an opportunity for complaint or criticism. Expressions of care might sound like:

I really regret that happened.

It makes me sad to hear about. . . .

I am very sorry. I know it must have hurt when. . . .

As directed by your facilitator, either share your responses with one or two participants or with the whole group. Be certain to express care as each member shares. Your caring words might sound like the examples given above. You may want to record these responses in the Team Journal at the end of the chapter.

Crises in the Results

Finally, the 21st century church is facing crises in its results. Consider the following:

- Almost 90 percent of churches in the Western world are stagnant, declining, or plateaued (Fuller, 1991).

- Of the ten percent of churches in the United States that are actually growing, less than one-third are growing by the conversion of unbelievers (Fuller, 1991).

- It is estimated that between 3,500 and 4,000 churches close each year in the United States. One of the fastest growing segments of the U.S. real estate market consists of churches that are being abandoned.

These statistics point to a disturbing reality in contemporary Western society, one that Dr. George Barna addresses concisely and convincingly: "Americans today are more devoted to seeking spiritual enlightenment than at any previous time during the twentieth century. Yet, at this moment of opportunity, Christianity is having less impact on people's perspectives and behaviors than ever. Why is that? Because a growing majority of people have dismissed the Christian faith as weak, outdated, and irrelevant" (Barna, 1998).

If we keep doing what we have been doing, we are going to keep getting the results we have been getting. The fact is that our churches are perfectly designed to achieve the results they are currently producing. Therefore, if we sense that God is satisfied with these results, we should continue with business as usual. But if we sense His displeasure, we must insist on change.

WHAT TYPE OF LEADERSHIP DO WE NEED?

If the church is to truly become an agent for effectively drawing the world to Christ, its leaders will have to embrace the life-changing impact that comes from intimately knowing Christ and fully experiencing what it means to be loved by Him. In other words, we must be relational leaders. A relational leader will know his or her own identity with certainty: "I am a person who is loved by God." Out of that identity, you can boldly declare what the Christian life is all about. We will not only be leaders who believe right doctrine and display right behavior, but leaders who also know how to love. The Spirit will sustain our ministry to others as we make a sacrificial commitment to tell the world, "We've been loved by the One who is love!"

Creating a church with a restored identity and restored relevance will require leaders of a different kind. It will require leaders who think beyond programmed events or competitive advantage. The 21st century church needs leaders whose focus is not solely on planning the next activity or offering the best opportunities for people. The church needs leaders who are not preoccupied with what other churches are doing and who do not strive to stay on the cutting edge of ministry merely to avoid falling behind in attendance or status. Finally, the church must have leaders who are personally prepared for the ministry ahead of them, fully equipped to minister first to their spouse and children and then to the congregation as a whole. Relational leadership is needed to help restore an identity of love to the 21st century church. But what is relational leadership?

Relational Leadership Defined

We define *relational leadership* as follows: "serving others to build a caring and connected team, which identifies and accomplishes significant and lasting objectives, as all are sacrificially committed to growth in love."

> *Relational leadership* is "serving others to build a caring and connected team, which identifies and accomplishes significant and lasting objectives, as all are sacrificially committed to growth in love."

This course will thoroughly explore what this definition actually means in the lives of leaders and those they lead. For the present, we will briefly expand each part of the above definition.

A Person: Called by God to Become a Servant. A relational leader is called by God to minister to others. This calling is more than a vocational choice or a preferred way of spending our time. Rather, it is a sense that God offers each of us the opportunity to utilize our gifts, talents, and life for His glory. Because relational leaders take this opportunity seriously, they will closely examine their preparedness to lead and serve others. They must possess certain spiritual and relational gifts and most certainly must discover their proper placement within the church. Some are called to minister the Word, and some are called to serve tables. Either way, all leaders serve, and all believers lead (see Acts 6:2-4; Gangel, 1981).

A Team: Caring and Connected. A relational leader works to build fellowship among a group of people "fitly joined together" through their experience of what the Bible calls fellowship or *koinonia*. Interestingly, there are two connotations of the word *koinonia,* each of which reveals a fundamental aspect of a caring and connected team. First, groups that experience *koinonia* learn to share their hearts and lives with one another vulnerably. Second, these people become committed partners in pursuit of a purpose centered on the divine and the eternal. True *koinonia* includes both the blessing of edifying relationships and the partnering together in God's Great Commission purpose (Hendriksen, 1962).

A Vision: For Eternal Priorities and Objectives. Out of the servant's heart comes a desire to build a connected and caring team. From the fellowship within this team comes the discernment, empowerment, and implementation of common vision for significant and lasting impact for the cause of Christ.

A Commitment to and Plan for Growth. The relational leader must first build a caring team and cast a vision for lasting, eternal objectives. But the relational leader must also commit to growth, including personal growth, the growth of other individuals, and ministry growth. We must realize, however, that growth is not primarily dependent upon what is said or how much is done. A plan for growth must not stop with developing better methods for communicating to people. It must not center on ways to conceive and present enticing events. It must not be concerned with erecting more attractive buildings. An effective growth plan must focus on spiritual and relational growth.

Personal Exercise #4

Review the four parts of the Relational Leadership definition and then ask yourself, "Which part of the definition might need to be strengthened in my own life?" Complete the following sentences:

As I look at my own leadership, the relational leadership concept that I need to strengthen is . . .

- *having a heart to serve others.*
- *building a caring and connected team.*
- *discerning and casting vision relationally.*
- *planning for growing myself, others, and our ministry in His love.*

I think God would want this change in me because . . .

Share your responses with one or two others, then pray together, asking God to strengthen you or change you in at least one area of leadership. You may want to record these responses in the Team Journal at the end of the chapter.

THE MOTIVATION FOR CHANGE: CHRIST'S STARTLING LOVE

In order for leaders to infuse this identity of love into the 21st century church, they will have to startle people with God's love. For leaders to even understand what that means, they will first have to experience the startling love of Jesus for themselves. Let us take a look at how Jesus startled the people He encountered.

First, Jesus said many startling things. As a young lad, He got lost in the intrigue of the synagogue and said to Mary and Joseph, "I must be about my Father's business." In His first sermon, Christ took a scroll of Isaiah and said, "The spirit of the Lord is upon me and is compelling me to preach the gospel." That certainly shocked those in attendance because He went on to explain, "Today, this Scripture has been fulfilled in your hearing." Jesus startled the lame man when He told him, "Rise and walk." Christ startled the blind men when He announced, "Your faith has made you well." The Savior filled His conversations with words that startled those around Him (see Luke 2:49; 4:16–21; 5:24; Matthew 9:29).

Jesus also did a lot of startling things. He surprised others when He broke social norms by talking to a Samaritan woman (John 4:7–26) and eating with tax collectors (Luke 19:5–7). He gave thoughtful recognition to widows (21:2–4) and children (Mark 10:14–16), and publicly criticized the arrogance of the well-placed, the well-educated, and the well-to-do. Christ's miracles were also undoubtedly startling to those around Him. He walked on water (Matthew 14:25) and turned water into wine (John 2:1–11). He healed people of disease (Luke 4:40), cured birth defects (Matthew 12:10–13), and even raised people from the dead (John 11:1–44). He calmed furious winds with the spoken word and commanded the billowing waves of the sea to cease (Mark 4:37–41).

Christ's words were startling and His miracles amazing, but what He said and what He did was primarily meant to call attention to how He loved. Take a moment and reflect on how Jesus loved people and how He startled them with His love.

Jesus startled the lepers by bringing healing to their bodies and dignity to their lives (Luke 17:12). As outcasts, they must have ached for the accepting touch of a family member, the warm embrace of a friend. Christ's healing touch brought restoration of both body and soul. Jesus startled a Samaritan woman when He broke all cultural conventions and asked for a drink of water (John 4:7). In the midst of her shame and her sense of having been rejected by her community, the Savior entrusted her with a conversation about things eternal. With His grace-filled eyes, Christ saw past her life choices and offered her His love. Jesus startled the woman caught in adultery when He knelt down beside her, joining her at the point of her hurt and providing protection for her life. Jesus' words dispersed her accusers and then offered restoration as He lovingly said, "Where are your accusers? Neither do I accuse you. Go and sin no more" (see John 8:3–11).

All the way to Calvary, Christ startled people with His love. Imagine Him hanging on the cross between heaven and earth, this One who knew no sin, absorbing all of the world's sin into Himself. Imagine how He must have startled those Roman soldiers—the ones who had driven nails into His hands, pierced His side, and tortured His body—as He looked at them and said, "Father, forgive them, for they do not know what they are doing (Luke 23:34)." Think about the thief who was crucified next to Christ. After a lifetime of deception, he must have been startled to hear the words, "Today you will be with Me in paradise" (v.43). Finally, Jesus looked down from the cross and saw His mother Mary standing with His beloved disciple John. Once again, He displayed His startling love. Looking ahead to His approaching death, He made provision for His mother by saying, "Mary, behold your son; John, behold your mother" (see John 19:26, 27). The Bible says that from that day forward, Mary lived in the house of John.

In your mind, picture Jesus in agony on the cross. He is prepared to take upon Himself the sins of the world. He will soon sense His own Father turn His back on Him, and will cry out, in a voice that conveys a feeling of utter abandonment: "My God, my God, why have you forsaken me?" (Mark 15:34). Yet there He hangs, still startling people with His love. He is the One dying, and yet He is thinking of everyone else. He is giving up His life, yet He is still giving of Himself so that others might know His love. That is the startling love of Christ. It is this startling love that we must first experience and then embody if we are to become relational leaders, leaders who will embrace the identity of the 1st century church while striving to revive and renew its 21st century descendant.

Experiencing the Word Together

"He who did not spare His own Son, but gave Him up for us all—how will He not also, along with Him, graciously give us all things" (Romans 8:32)?

Imagine Christ hanging on the cross. He is preparing to die. He's taking on the sins of the world, about to do battle with the forces of evil, yet He is thinking of someone else. That someone else is you. Christ has been beaten and tortured, but He's thinking of your hurts and your pain. Jesus is about to provide redemption for all of mankind, yet He's mindful of you and your concerns. He's interested in your life, your circumstances, and your salvation. Christ is about to die because He wants a relationship with you. What does it do to your heart to consider all that Jesus endured, and to recognize that He did it for you?

As I reflect on God's gift for me in the death of His Son, and consider that He did it because He wants a relationship with me, I feel _____ *because . . .*

Share your feelings with your partner or small group, then take turns giving thanks to God in prayer. Pray a prayer of gratitude that Jesus died just for you!

Now, take a moment and consider how you might have experienced the love of Jesus in addition to Calvary. When have you sensed the startling, surprising love of Christ for you? What other things has God graciously given to you? Take a moment to pray and ask God to bring to your mind an example that brings gratefulness to your heart. Did He startle you with His healing? With His acceptance? Did Jesus surprise you with His forgiveness or amaze you with His restoration? Did He startle you with His provision or a reassurance of His presence?

Consider how you might complete the following sentence:

I recall a time when I _____ *, and Jesus startled me with His love.*

Share your response with your partner or small group. Celebrate the gracious gifts of Jesus' love for you.

My Team Journal

■ What insights did you gain as a result of this session? What did you come to know about the individuals in your team?

_____

_____

_____

_____

_____

■ What did each person share about their desires for more expressions of the identity of the 1st century church? These responses will give you insight into how to express the "startling love of Christ" to each team member.

Name: Responses:

_____

_____

_____

_____

■ What did each team member share about the painful impact of church leaders? How have they been negatively affected by secular approaches to leadership?

Name: Responses:

_____

_____

_____

_____

■ What leadership concept did each person want to strengthen? What does each person want to do differently?

Name: Responses:

_____

_____

_____

_____

■ Given all you have come to know about your team, how might you better love each one?

Name: Ways I can love them:

_____

_____

_____

_____

Chapter 1 Outline

I. Why Do We Need a Different Type of Leadership?

A. The Crisis of Identity in the Church

   1. What did the 1st century church have that appears to be missing in the 21st century church?

   2. How do you think non-Christians today would answer the question, "Who are Christians?"

Personal Exercise #1

B. Crises Among Church Leaders

   1. What kinds of problems do we see today among Christian leaders?

   2. Have you or someone you know been hurt by a leader's moral/ethical failure? By a divorce or other breakdown in a leader's family? By a leader who was suffering from burnout?

Personal Exercise #2

C. Crises in Our Approaches to Leadership

   1. Secular approaches to leadership brought into Christian leadership:
     a. Chief executive officer
     b. Classic management: "Get things done through people."
     c. Management by committee
     d. "Do what everyone else is doing."

   2. Have you ever been negatively affected by leaders who used one of these approaches within a church or ministry?

Personal Exercise #3

D. Crises in the Results

   1. Almost 90 percent of churches in the Western world are declining or "plateaued."

   2. Of the ten percent of churches that are growing, only a very small percentage of them actually increase by "conversion growth."

   3. An estimated 3,500–4,000 churches will close in America this year.

   4. People are increasingly open to spiritual things, but are increasingly less interested in Christianity.

II. What Type of Leadership Do We Need?

A. A Person: Called by God to Become a Servant

   1. Example of servant leadership in Acts 6

   2. All leaders serve (some serve tables, some serve the Word).

B. A Team: Caring and Connected

   1. Fellowship/*koinonia*: sharing our lives with each other

   2. Sharing as partners with purpose

C. A Vision: For Eternal Priorities and Objectives

   1. Vision for what matters: the cause of Christ

   2. Vision developed within the team (not by just one leader)

D. A Commitment to and Plan for Growth

   1. Both individually and collectively as a team

   2. Not simply by what we say or do, but by startling people with His love

Personal Exercise #4

III. The Motivation for Change: Christ's Startling Love

Experiencing the Word Together

My Team Journal

Additional Resources

George Barna, *The Second Coming of the Church* (Nashville, TN: Word Publishing, 1998).

The Fuller Institute of Church Growth Report (Pasadena, CA: 1991).

Kenneth O. Gangel, *Building Leadership for Church Education* (Chicago, IL: Moody Press, 1981).

William Hendriksen, *Exposition of Philippians* (Grand Rapids, MI: Baker, 1962).

John Kotter, *Leading Change* (Boston, MA: Harvard Business School Press, 1996).

Richard Kriegbaum, *Leadership Prayers* (Wheaton, IL: Tyndale House, 1998).

H.B. London, Jr. and Neil B. Wiseman, *Pastors at Risk* (Wheaton, IL: Chariot Victor Books, 1993).

Tom Marshall, *Understanding Leadership* (Grand Rapids, MI: Baker Book House, 2003).

Reggie McNeal, ed. *Revolution in Leadership* (Nashville, TN: Abingdon Press, 1998).

James Means, *Effective Pastors for a New Century* (Grand Rapids, MI: Baker, 1993).

Stewart Snook, *Developing Leaders—Case Studies from Africa* (Wheaton, IL: Billy Graham Center, 1992).

Lovett H. Weems, *Leadership in the Wesleyan Spirit* (Nashville: Abingdon Press, 1999).

Walter C. Wright, Jr., *Relational Leadership: A Biblical Model for Influence and Service* (Carlisle, England: Paternoster Press, 2002).

Chapter 2

Developing Our Identity as Relational Leaders: Becoming Servants

The crises in the church today demand change. Our strategies and methodologies for ministry must change in order to more effectively meet the needs of contemporary society. We must also consider changing our presentation of the Gospel (while recognizing that the *message* of the Gospel always stays the same) if it is to have any relevance for the unchurched world. But most of all, the church of today must recover its identity. We must move from an identity of spiritual dogmatism to an identity of a people of love. It stands to reason then that we, as leaders of the church, will have to revamp our own identity as well. Since the way we lead is an expression of who we are, we must question who we need to become.

Let us consider a time when Jesus addressed this very question of identity in a private time with His disciples. The Passover was a sacred commemoration, a time when the Jewish nation celebrated God's gracious covenant love. The Feast of Unleavened Bread was to be a consistent reminder of God's redemption of Israel from bondage in Egypt. Jesus' Passover meal with His disciples was even more special than usual. Jesus longed to eat this supper with His friends because He knew it would be the last one He would share with them before His death.

Christ came to the meal with a heavy heart. His remaining days on earth were few, and time with His disciples was short. Jesus began the meal with vulnerability. He told His friends how much this meal meant to Him and revealed His destiny of suffering and pain when He said, "I have eagerly desired to eat this Passover with you before I suffer. For I tell you, I will not eat it again until it finds fulfillment in the kingdom of God." Jesus then led the disciples through the sacred remembrances of Passover. He broke the bread, gave thanks to God, and then vulnerably revealed to the disciples, "This is my body given for you; do this in remembrance of me." The Savior told His closest friends that His body was about to be sacrificed, given up, and broken for them. Christ then took the cup and said, "This cup is the new covenant in my blood, which is poured out for you," further revealing what lay ahead. With one final measure of vulnerability, Jesus ended the Passover meal by delivering the tragic news that one of the twelve would betray Him (Luke 22:14–30).

On this somber note, the Passover meal ended. Jesus' heart was resolute, yet filled with sadness. The Savior was hurting, grieving, and preparing to die. His friends' response to His pain no doubt added to His sorrow. Luke tells us that moments after Jesus had told them what was to happen, "A dispute arose among them as to which of them was considered to be greatest" (v. 24).

Jesus revealed the tender places of His heart, and yet His friends, the future leaders of the church, began to squabble over which of them was the greatest. Their focus was on their own position and status rather than on Him. Jesus responded to the disciples' ill-timed and insensitive concerns in the midst of His own heartache. From a saddened heart, Christ gave instruction about becoming great in God's kingdom. He contrasted the world's view of greatness with the Father's perspective and warned the disciples not to lead like the Gentiles, with their hierarchal systems and competitive focus (vv. 24–26).

Imagine yourself with Jesus and the disciples in the upper room. The Savior is vulnerable, hurting, and soon to be betrayed, but the disciples are arguing over who is to be the greatest. Christ has just shared that He is going to suffer, give up His body, and shed His blood, yet the disciples begin to quarrel with one another. As you imagine this scene, try to feel the insensitivity in their response. Begin to sense the pain the Savior must have experienced.

> **Relational leaders are motivated by a desire to serve, not a desire to lead.**

Experiencing the Word Together #1

"I want to know Christ and the power of his resurrection and the fellowship of sharing in his sufferings" (Philippians 3:10).

Take a moment to reflect on what the disciples' response did to the Savior's heart. Imagine how He must have felt. Begin to *know Him* and how He must have suffered, even in the upper room. How might you complete the following statement?

I imagine that Christ may have felt . . .

Now, consider His plea and how it might shape your view of leadership. Imagine Christ in His sorrow, sharing these words: "I see how the world's leaders treat those they lead, but you are not to lead like that."

Pause to consider the heart of Christ, this One who is acquainted with sorrow and grief, as you hear Him utter these words: "Let it not be so among you." Is it possible that this is still the Savior's heart cry? Could He still be longing to see a difference in how His disciples lead people?

Reflect now on what it does to *your* heart that Jesus, the One who was wounded for our transgressions, experienced these hurts. Truly begin to fellowship with Him in His suffering. What does it do to your heart as you reflect on all that Jesus must have felt in the upper room? What do you feel *for Him*?

As I consider Christ's sorrow, my heart is touched with . . .

Share those feelings with one or two other participants. You may want to record these reponses in the Team Journal at the end of the chapter.

As you finish sharing with one another, spend a few moments praying together. Share your heart with the Lord. Tell Jesus of your desire to truly know Him. Tell Christ about your care, sadness, and hurt for Him. Ask Him to make you a leader who is different from the world, a leader like Himself.

RELATIONAL LEADERS DO NOT STRIVE TO BECOME LEADERS.

Now that our hearts have been sensitized to the pain Christ must have felt, let us take a look at how His words to the disciples have meaning and application today.

The disciples' response was hurtful and insensitive, but not surprising, since they lived in a culture built on a rigid hierarchy of leadership and a strict adherence to social class distinctions. Leadership in the secular culture was built on power, status, authority, and competitive advantage. Unfortunately, the religious community was no different. The Pharisees employed a leadership style that was influenced more by their Roman rulers than by the God of their forefathers. Even Christ's closest companions missed the mark when it came to leadership. The disciples expected to lead with the same competitive predisposition as their contemporaries. They assumed they should work hard to climb the ladder of status and attain success in Christ's kingdom. The Savior revealed His very different perspective on leadership in the upper room when He told the disciples that while they were to be "in the world," they were not to be "of it" (John 17:15–19). His message to the disciples that evening remains the same for us today: "Don't lead like the world leads. Don't strive for greatness. Don't pursue status. Don't seek to become a leader!"

You may be asking yourself, "How can I possibly become a relational leader if I do not strive to become a leader at all? What is the problem with wanting to lead?" There are several potential pitfalls to consider.

We May Become Filled With Pride.

The person who pursues leadership runs a serious risk of developing a preoccupation with self that can hurt others. The disciples certainly illustrated this risk as their own preoccupation with greatness hurt our Savior.

Jesus addressed the issue of pride on another occasion when He spoke to "some who were confident of their own righteousness and looked down on everybody else" (Luke 18:9). In the parable He told that day, Jesus contrasted the haughtiness of the Pharisee with the humility of the tax collector. Christ explained that the tax collector went home "justified before God" (v. 14) because of his humility and gave warning that "everyone who exalts himself will be humbled" (v. 14).

Proverbs 13:10 further cautions us about the dangers of prideful living: "Pride only breeds quarrels." That warning is important for us today because anyone who strives to become a leader may grow so proud that he or she is more intent on being "right" than on doing right things. Pride can make a leader more concerned with "doing the job" than building relationships, more driven by personal success than by a longing to express tender-hearted care. Indeed, a pride-filled leader may have the tendency to use people to accomplish his or her own goals rather than seeking to serve them. This self-centered, success-driven approach to leadership, with its indifference toward the needs and feelings of others, will inevitably breed conflict between the leader and the led, just as Proverbs warns.

We May Become Defensive.

Individuals who pursue leadership often feel threatened by or jealous of other people and respond with defensiveness and tight control. This type of leader must always be in charge in order to guard his or her position, and may even attack any who pose a threat.

King Saul illustrated this tendency when he became enraged because of the people's admiration of David. Scripture tells us that "Saul was very angry . . . 'What more can he get but the kingdom?' And from that time on Saul kept a jealous eye on David" (1 Samuel 18:6–9). Saul's defensiveness and jealousy became so severe that he physically attacked David: "Saul tried to pin him to the wall with his spear, but David eluded him as Saul drove the spear into the wall" (19:10). King Saul's jealousy drove him to attack and his defensiveness compelled him to send David into battle, yet beneath all of these behaviors, Scripture tells us that Saul was actually afraid of David (18:12–21).

This same sense of fear and anxiety often underlies the behavior of a defensive leader. A jealous or controlling leader is usually a fearful leader. He or she may fear a loss of status, position, attention, or value, and those who seek to follow this kind of leader may bear the brunt of his or her insecurities. Such leaders have missed an essential element of biblical leadership, namely that leaders and elders in the body of Christ are challenged to be approachable and teachable (Titus 1:6–9).

We May Become Ungrateful.

Individuals who set out to accomplish the goal of becoming leaders may only have themselves to thank for their achievements and successes. While gaining temporary satisfaction from their efforts, these leaders can quickly become preoccupied with keeping accounts, maintaining a running tally of all they have done for others and all that is owed in return. An attitude of entitlement can result from an ungrateful heart as the leader expects other people, or even God, to "do for me" because of "all I have done for you."

The children of Israel give us insight into this type of leader. A generation of Israelites crossed the Red Sea on dry ground, was fed in the desert by God Himself, and witnessed countless miracles. Yet Moses tells us that these future leaders forgot the blessings of the Lord and began to wish for a return to the captivity of Egypt (Numbers 14:1–4). Those ungrateful Israelites who failed to give thanks to God suffered for 40 years in the desert, and ultimately missed out on the blessings of the Promised Land. The Lord warned their leaders about taking credit for any success: "You may say to yourself, 'My power and the strength of my hands have produced this wealth for me.' But remember the Lord your God, for it is He who gives you the ability to produce wealth" (Deuteronomy 8:17, 18). We must take heed from the example of the children of Israel because God tells us that "Everything that was written in the past was written to teach us, so that through endurance and the encouragement of the Scriptures we might have hope" (Romans 15:4).

We must also consider one other implication of ungratefulness. Many leaders today may work out of a sense duty or obligation as their ungrateful hearts say, "Look how hard I have worked; it all depends on me," rather than, "Look how much God has done for us; it all depends upon Him!" As a result of such thinking, individuals who strive to become leaders can become easily wearied by the obligations of ministry since they have so few inner resources to sustain the joy of serving others.

Personal Exercise #1

Consider your own experiences with different leaders. Have you been around leaders who seemed to be focused on becoming a leader? Did you eventually become aware of their pride? Have you been exposed to their defensiveness, control, or jealousy? Have you encountered their sense of obligation, entitlement, or weariness of ministry?

What impact did this person have on you? What response did that produce in you?

Complete the following sentence. As you share with other participants, leave out names or details that would identify a specific leader.

I have experienced the negative results that come from striving to be a leader. I was affected or impacted in the following ways . . .

As directed by your facilitator, share your responses with one or two other participants or with a small group. You may want to record these responses in the Team Journal at the end of the chapter.

As you completed the exercise above, you undoubtedly uncovered many painful wounds inflicted by individuals who have striven to become leaders. Let us take a look at the relational leader's alternative approach.

RELATIONAL LEADERS SEEK TO BECOME SERVANTS.

Jesus, our perfect model of leadership, told us what a leader ought to be. When He spoke to the disciples in the upper room, He urged and exemplified servant leadership, saying, "I am among you as One who serves" (Luke 22:27). In response to their prideful preoccupation with success, Christ told them that servanthood is the key to greatness in God's kingdom. He then proceeded to model the kind of servant leadership that He was encouraging them to embrace. "After that, he poured water into a basin and began to wash His disciples' feet" (John 13:5). Jesus challenged His disciples to follow His example when He told them, "Now that I, your Lord and Teacher have washed your feet, you also should wash one another's feet" (v. 14).

How revolutionary! The disciples had expressed the model of leadership with which they were all too familiar: greatness equals "being in charge" and having others serve you. By contrast, Jesus told them that in order to become truly great, one must serve. Likewise, if we are to become relational leaders, we cannot strive for power and notoriety or set our sights on success. A relational leader pursues a different goal—an identity of servanthood.

If we are to successfully make this shift from pursuing a position of leadership to aspiring to an identity of servanthood, we must become well-acquainted with the identifying marks of a servant. As we pursue the following servant characteristics, those we lead will be blessed, our ministry will be strengthened, and our God will be loved.

Servants Display Humility.

A humble heart is the first mark of the servant. A servant leader is defined by a critical concern for the needs of others and consistently lives out the biblical mandate to "think more highly of others than himself" (see Philippians 2:3). He or she strives to find ways to meet the needs of others rather than constantly pursuing personal success or achievement. Humble leaders are free to think of others because they are confident that God is thinking of them. Because the Lord takes care of even the lilies of the field, humble servants

> **Servants are characterized by humility, faith, and gratitude.**

recognize their value to Him, and rest in the assurance that the Great Provider is mindful of and able to supply for their needs (Matthew 6:28–34).

As we pursue an identity of servanthood, we must look to the divine Servant as our model of humility. Jesus exemplified humility as He took the towel and basin of water and washed the disciples' feet. Christ, the King of kings, demonstrated a humble spirit as He rode into Jerusalem on a lowly donkey rather than a majestic stallion or royal chariot. The Son of God made a declaration of His humility when He said, "I do nothing on my own, but speak just what the Father has taught me" (John 8:28). And with loving words, Christ reaffirmed His humility and invited us to join Him: "Come to me, all you who are weary and burdened, and I will give you rest. Take my yoke upon you and learn from me, for I am gentle and humble in heart" (Matthew 11:28, 29).

When leaders pursue an identity of servanthood, their humility is readily revealed in their actions. Humility describes Reverend Al and his wife, Jan. These two leaders followed God's call upon their lives to leave the security of a secular business for the unpredictability of church ministry. Every member of their church is extremely grateful for their decision because they have all been personally blessed by Al and Jan's ministry. Reverend Al displays humility each time he invites a church member to lunch. His congregation knows that an invitation for lunch does not mean that Al wants to ask for their help or a contribution to the ministry. He just wants to get to know them. Families have been blessed when Jan provides a meal and emotional support during a time of family crisis. They feel the extent of her love and are amazed at her wisdom, but they never hear Jan call attention to her efforts or take credit for the help. She just gives without expectation of acknowledgement or reward. Al and Jan can be found in the "unlikely places" of leadership, those places without spotlight or platform. They can often be seen doing yard work for an elderly church member or lending a hand with the children when there has been a death in the family. Those they lead always sense their willingness to serve through the demonstrations of love they share. Al and Jan often speak vulnerably of how God is convicting and changing them, acknowledging His constant work in their own lives.

In addition to their actions, humble leaders can also be distinguished by the words they say and the messages they convey. A humble leader brings attention to all that God is doing rather than calling attention to his or her own efforts. He or she points the congregation to God's handiwork, God's grace, and God's provision rather than referring to "my work," "my ministry," or "my church." In doing so, the humble leader conveys the attitude, "This is not about me. This is about Him!" Servant leaders with humble hearts willingly acknowledge a need for, and dependence on, God, as well as a need for human relationships.

Servants Demonstrate Faith.

Expectant faith is the second mark of the servant. As mentioned before, humble leaders are free to think of others as more important than themselves because they are confident of God's care on their behalf. Similarly, servant leaders make it a priority to look for God's handiwork in their lives. They look for how the Father has provided, how He has intervened, and how He has displayed His great power in His dealings with them. Faith-filled leaders recognize that God knows and cares about our needs. As we then, by faith, humbly express our needs to God, He is allowed to demonstrate His love for us. True servant leaders develop such confidence in God's tender care that it blossoms into unshakeable faith. A faithful leader looks to God to accomplish goals and maintains a God-centered perspective that looks far beyond all that man can do.

In order to become a faith-filled leader, we must look to the One who inspires our faith and trust. Jesus demonstrated His own humility, dependency, and faith in the Father as He performed many of His miracles. They give us a glimpse of the Savior's faith in the Father's knowledge of and care for people's needs. Before Jesus fed the five thousand on the hills of Galilee, He looked to heaven and prayed. By first giving thanks to the Father, Jesus declared His humble dependency and expressed absolute faith in His Father's provision (Matthew 14:15–21). Christ also demonstrated faith when He raised Lazarus from the grave (John 11:1–44). Jesus openly expressed His trust in God, allowing everyone present that day to hear Him. He said, "Father, I thank you that you have heard me. I knew that you always hear me, but I said this for the benefit of the people standing here, that they may believe" (vv. 41, 42).

The relational leader will also demonstrate faith in observable ways. Faith exhibits itself in quiet confidence even in the midst of challenge or difficulty. Relational leaders will demonstrate faith similar to that of King Jehoshaphat, who looked at the overwhelming military force arrayed against Jerusalem and said, "We do not know what to do, but our eyes are upon you" (2 Chronicles 20:12). Faith also manifests itself as freedom from defensiveness and fearful control. A faith-filled leader will accept change and willingly hear the concerns of others, confident of God's sovereign plan. We see faith displayed when leaders live to see how God will show up rather than defending certain positions or trying to manipulate or pressure others toward particular opinions.

The relational leader will have an expectant heart like that of our Savior, and others will be able to hear the words that validate that faith. This expectancy of faith cries out, "I believe this will happen; I am confident God can do it." A faith-filled heart declares what can be done rather than explaining all the reasons why things will not work.

Larry and Sharon Evans certainly express their faith and expectant heart to the couples' class of their church. Larry's cancer diagnosis was the turning point for the Evans. The disease shook their marriage, their family, and their security in ways they had never dreamed possible. But as God demonstrated His great healing in Larry's life, the Evans began to tell of God's provision and their faith in Him. This testimony of faith now permeates their ministry to the couples of their church. They help each couple through the obstacles and challenges of life with a quiet confidence in what God can do. Whether it is legal issues that seem insurmountable or the painful heartache of children who stray from their convictions, the Evans share their hope and faith in how God can abundantly provide in people's lives. Because of their faith in Christ, the Evans can minister with great confidence and freedom. They do not worry about losing their ministry or feel threatened by other influential leaders in their church. They know that the same God who demonstrated His love and healing power in their personal lives can change, sustain, or provide for those they serve.

Servants Are Empowered by Gratitude.

Gratitude is the third characteristic of servant leaders. In humility, the relational leader thinks of others because he or she is confident of God's provision. In faith, the relational leader knows God will provide or demonstrate His power because he or she consistently looks for the Lord's compassionate care. But what is it that provides the motivation, the empowerment, for being a servant? As the servant leader reflects on all that God has done, his or her heart is filled with an overwhelming sense of gratitude. Relational leaders are filled with the awe and wonder of who God is. They are overwhelmed not only by the miraculous things He has done, but also by the fact that they get to be a part of all He is doing!

As we pursue the goal of servanthood, we must look again to the Savior and the testimony of His Word to prompt our hearts to gratitude. Even the Son, who lives eternally in the mystery of the Trinity, proclaimed His gratitude and love for the Father. Jesus declared with a grateful heart, "As the Father has loved Me, so have I loved you" (John 15:9). Christ announced His gratitude and admiration for the Father as He proclaimed the believers' confidence: "My Father, who has given them to me, is greater than all; no one can snatch them out of my Father's hand" (10:29). Finally, Jesus told us that His obedience to the Father is connected to His gratefulness for the Father's love. "The Son can do nothing by himself; he can only do what He sees his Father doing, because whatever the Father does the Son also does. For the Father loves the Son and shows him all he does" (5:19, 20). The apostle Paul helped us see this same connection between gratitude and obedience. "It is the love of Christ (and gratefulness for it) that controls me" (see 2 Corinthians 5:14).

God gives us a promise of sustained energy and increased strength as we lead others in ministry, but we must first abide in His command: "Praise the Lord, O my soul, and **forget not** all his benefits—[He forgives . . . He heals . . . He redeems . . . He crowns you with love and satisfies your desires] **so that** your youth is renewed like the eagle's" (Psalm 103:2). God's Word tells us that as we are grateful to Him, we experience more of His blessings according to our needs. Scripture also reveals that our gratefulness and thanksgiving is key to worship, important for answered prayer, and critical for entering the presence of God (Hebrews 12:28; Philippians 4:6; Psalm 100:4).

Gratitude is vital for the relational leader because it guards against the burdens of weariness, drudgery, and duty in ministry. Gratitude empowers the servant's heart, helping to sustain the joy of serving others, lest it become reluctant obligation. A grateful heart says, "I cannot get over the fact that I get to do this. I am so glad I get to be a fellow-worker with Jesus Christ" (see 1 Corinthians 3:9).

Janna's life and work are a testimony to her gratefulness. She lives in a large metropolitan city and coordinates a ministry she has named *Rebecca's House*. Janna began *Rebecca's House* out of gratitude for the tremendous investment that a woman named Rebecca made in her life. When Janna was 19, she found herself pregnant, homeless, and completely alone in a scary and unfamiliar place. Rebecca, an elderly woman, offered Janna a warm meal, a warm embrace, and a warm place to live. The two ladies became like family to one another, and because of Rebecca's testimony, Janna became a child of the King. Now, years later, Janna directs a ministry for other pregnant teenagers and unwed mothers. It is her life's mission to provide the same warmth and care that Rebecca provided for her. Janna faces daily challenges and obstacles in her pursuit, but despite the lack of financial resources, the shortage of volunteers, and the multiple needs of those she serves, Janna is sustained because she remembers the tender love of God that touched her life through her friend, Rebecca. It is her gratitude to the Lord for His many blessings that keeps her going.

Personal Exercise #2

Think again about your experience with the leaders in your life. Have you had the blessing of being around leaders who truly demonstrated servant leadership? Were you blessed by their humility? Impressed by their expressions of faith? Awed by their grateful heart?

What positive impact did this person have on you? How did you respond?

I have been blessed because someone in my life displayed servant leadership, particularly an expression of _____. I was impacted in the following ways:

As directed by your facilitator, share your responses with one or two other participants or with a small group. You may want to record these responses in the Team Journal at the end of the chapter.

As you completed the previous exercise, you undoubtedly identified many of the blessings that come when others lead like Jesus. Those leaders had a positive impact on your life as they continued to become humble, faith-filled, and grateful. Likewise, as we pursue our goal of becoming servants, we will want those same characteristics to describe who we are becoming.

As you and I begin to valiantly pursue this goal of becoming a servant, what will sustain our efforts? What will motivate us to keep on serving when the inevitable challenges of leadership come our way? When those we are serving are too needy or too critical, what will help us keep our focus and leave us undeterred in our pursuit of servanthood?

Self-discipline alone will not enable us to accomplish our goal. Sheer determination will not keep us on track. How will we carry on?

As relational leaders, we must develop a different motivation that will sustain our servant identity. We will only be driven to pursue our goal of servanthood by being overwhelmed and awestruck by the opportunity we have to startle Jesus with our love.

THE ULTIMATE MOTIVATION OF THE RELATIONAL LEADER: THE OPPORTUNITY TO LOVE GOD

We have discussed the necessity of restoring an identity of love to the 21st century church and the fact that such a restoration will come only if we have leaders who know *how* to love. So where do we start? First, we must recall often how Jesus has startled us with His love. Relational leaders then begin "startling" Jesus with their love. We start by loving Him as we have been loved (1 John 4:19).

Consider this: our expressions of faith, humility, and gratitude are ways that we demonstrate our love for God. As we humbly submit ourselves to Him and acknowledge our dependency, we care for Him. As we live our lives with an expectant heart and faith-filled eyes, we bless the Lord. And as we express our gratitude for who He is and what He has done, He is loved! Faith, humility, and gratitude are all a part of how we live out the Great Commandment, to love God with all of our heart, soul, and mind (Matthew 22:37).

Loving God Through Humility

Jesus revealed how God's heart is moved by our expressions of humility. Christ gave special commendation to a widow as she gave two small coins to the temple treasury. As He sat in the temple teaching and preaching, He offered a special warning to His disciples. They were to beware of the prideful and hypocritical teachers who "walked around in flowing robes and loved to have the most important seats in the synagogue and the places of honor at banquets." In contrast, Jesus must have smiled when He looked across the temple and called the disciples' attention to the widow at the money box. It was her humility and her total dependency upon God that warranted Christ's approval. She gave all she had, yet she made no attempt to call attention to her offering (Mark 12:38–44).

The widow, unlike the religious leaders, apparently knew how to love the Lord. In her humility, she blessed God. In the same way, our humility brings joy to the heart of Christ. After all, the Bible reminds us that God resists the proud but gives grace to the humble (James 4:6).

Loving God Through Faith

The faith-filled leader understands that God's heart is hurt when His children are filled with doubt about His love. Remember the apostle's admonition in Hebrews: "Without faith, it is impossible to please God" (Hebrews 11:6). Christ's response to the centurion showed that a faith-filled servant is pleasing to God. As Jesus entered Capernaum, He received a message from a Roman centurion who was quite concerned for the health of his servant. The soldier sent a request for Christ to heal the servant, and exemplified faith when he said, "Lord, don't trouble yourself, for I do not deserve to have you come under my roof. . . . But say the word, and my servant will be healed." Scripture then tells us that the Holy One of Israel, the Savior of the universe, *was amazed* at the centurion. Jesus turned to the crowds that followed Him and revealed His astonishment: "I tell you, I have not found such great faith even in Israel" (Luke 7:1–10).

In the same way, when we live with an expectant heart for what God can do, and trust that His motives are always for our good, He is amazed, astonished, and loved by us. It undoubtedly brings joy to God's heart when we are sure that He will answer and confident that He will provide. Relational leaders demonstrate expectant faith because they are confident of God's heart of love, and, in turn, they bring pleasure to the Lord.

Loving God Through Gratitude

Finally, God is loved when we express our gratefulness to Him. Christ confirmed this truth when He healed the ten lepers. The Gospel of Luke tells us that these men made their way from the city and with a measure of faith began to say, "Master, have mercy on us." Jesus responded to their plea with compassion and told them to go and show themselves to the priest. As the lepers traveled toward Jerusalem, they were healed. The ten must have quickened their steps toward the purification ceremony that would have restored them back to fellowship with family and friends (see Leviticus 13–15). Curiously though, one of the ten men reversed direction. He stopped his journey to Jerusalem and turned back to express gratitude to Jesus. The Scriptures say that the man came back praising God in a loud voice. He threw himself at Jesus' feet and thanked Him. Then, most important, we read of Christ's response to the man: "Were not all ten cleansed? Where are the other nine?" What does this tell us about the heart of Jesus and the importance of a gratitude-filled heart? Apparently, it was painful for the Savior to see only one of the men return and express his gratefulness. There was only one out of the ten who knew how to love God—the one who expressed his love by returning to Jesus and giving thanks (Luke 17:11–19).

In much the same way, if we are going to pursue an identity of love, then we, too, will have to become like the one leper who returned, so overcome with gratitude that he could not stand to take one more step away from Jesus. As we offer praises and thanksgiving to God in a loud voice, His heart is blessed. He is loved when His children remember to express gratitude for who He is and how He provides.

Faith, humility, and gratitude are ways of manifesting our love for God, and these expressions of love fulfill a longing inside every created being. In fact, this is why we were created—to love Him! The Scriptures explain the sense of fulfillment that comes from expressing our love for God: "It is for thy good pleasure all things were created" (see Revelation 4:11). And He is worthy to receive all glory, honor and power.

Take a few moments now, and reflect on how you might better express your love for God.

Experiencing the Word Together #2

"On Him we have set our hope . . . as you help us by your prayers" (2 Corinthians 1:10, 11).

As you think about the traits of a relational leader—humility, faith, gratitude—which of these might God want to more deeply cultivate in your heart?

I think God would want to express more _____ (*humility, faith,* or *gratitude*) *through me, particularly concerning . . .*

Gather with two or three others, share your responses with one another, and pray together. You may want to record these responses in the Team Journal at the end of the chapter. Humble yourself as others pray for God to bring this change about in you. Tell God that you have great hope for change in each person's life because of His power.

Your prayers for one another might sound similar to the following:

God, may You fill this friend with humility and the heart of a servant. Through the ministry of the Holy Spirit, show him areas where You have resisted because of his pride. Open doors now and give grace when he is humble (James 4:6). *May he bring joy to your heart, Father. May he startle You with his humility and bless You with his love.*

God, may You fill this friend with confidence and faith in You. May she be overwhelmed by the Holy Spirit's power in her life and demonstrations of love on her behalf and then boldly proclaim her assurance of what You can do. May she please You because of her unshakable faith in You (Hebrews 11:6). *May she startle You with her faith and bless You with her love.*

God, may You grant this friend an overwhelming sense of gratitude for who You are and what You have done on his behalf. May he see and recognize Your efforts and then be motivated to serve because of a grateful heart that longs to lead like Jesus. May the Holy Spirit consistently work in his life so that he never forgets to give thanks for what You have done (Psalm 103:2). *May he startle You with his gratitude and bless You with his love.*

As God begins to answer these prayers and you become more humble, faith-filled, or grateful, your deepened love for the Lord will motivate your service to others.

In order to understand how this will happen, reflect again on the empathy that you felt for Christ at the beginning of this chapter. As you identified the painful experiences and personal disappointments He must have felt, your heart was moved with compassion. Would you have wanted to do something other than what the disciples did? Wouldn't it be wonderful if you could respond differently to Jesus? Wouldn't it be wonderful if you could respond with love?

Christ has a mysterious opportunity for us all. He told us, "Whatever you do for one of the least of these, you do for Me" (see Matthew 25:40). In other words, Christ might say to you and me, "When you prioritize the hurting person in your life, you are prioritizing Me. When you sit with your friend and comfort their pain, you are comforting Me. When you love someone in spite of their sin, you are loving Me." Relational leaders live out the mystery of "startling Jesus with their love," and then, in turn, express love for God as they love others.

> **Relational leaders are motivated by the opportunity to love Jesus.**

Learning how to lead others and lead them well will be our contribution to restoring the identity of love to the 21st century church. As relational leaders, we begin by loving God through our demonstrations of humility, faithfulness, and gratitude. Out of this love for Him and an experience of being loved by Him, our hearts will overflow with sacrificial love for other people. It is only this heart of love that will sustain our ministry as leaders, and only this kind of love that will begin to restore the true identity of the church as a people who love one another.

My Team Journal

■ What insights did you gain as a result of this session? What did you come to know about the individuals in your team?

_____

_____

_____

_____

■ Were you and your team able to express compassion for Christ? How did the experience of suffering with Jesus impact you and your team?

Name: Responses:

_____

_____

_____

_____

■ Think about the experiences your team has had with other leaders. How has each member been impacted by the negative traits of their leaders? What blessings have members experienced because of a relationship with a servant leader?

Name: Responses:

_____

_____

_____

_____

■ Which of the three traits (humility, faith, or gratitude) did each member want God to develop in their life? Why was this trait mentioned?

Name: Responses:

■ How might God want to change you as a result of this session? How might you startle Him with your faith? Your humility? Your gratitude?

Chapter 2 Outline

Experiencing the Word Together #1

I. Relational Leaders Do Not Strive to Become Leaders.
  A. We May Become Filled With Pride.
    1. Like the disciples, we may tend to put the focus on us.
    2. We may become driven by the pursuit of "personal success."
  B. We May Become Defensive.
    1. Easily threatened or jealous
    2. Having to be "in charge" in order to guard our position
    3. Saul with David (1 Samuel 18:6–9)
  C. We May Become Ungrateful.
    1. "I accomplished it, so I am grateful . . . to me!"
    2. "Because of all I've done for you, you owe me!"
    3. "It all depends on me!"

Personal Exercise #1

II. Relational Leaders Seek to Become Servants.
  A. Servants Display Humility.
    1. Concern for the needs of others (Philippians 2:3)
    2. Jesus as the model (Matthew 11:29)
      a. Washing feet (John 13:1–17)
      b. Riding into Jerusalem on a donkey (Luke 19:28–34)
      c. Depending completely upon His Father (John 8:28)
    3. Calling attention to what God has done rather than what a leader has done
  B. Servants Demonstrate Faith.
    1. Confident of God's care (1 Peter 5:7)
    2. Like Jesus: thanking his Father even before He performs the miracles
    (Matthew 14:15–21; John 11:41, 42)

3. Like King Jehoshaphat: confidence in God, looking for how God will "show up": "We do not know what to do, but our eyes are upon you" (2 Chronicles 20:12).
4. Declaring in faith, "I believe God can do it!"

C. Servants Are Empowered by Gratitude.
   1. The "awe and wonder" of what God has done, who He is, and that we get to be part of all He is doing
   2. Gratefulness guards against weariness.
      a. Grateful for the privilege of being "God's fellow workers" (1 Corinthians 3:9)
      b. "Praise the Lord . . . Forget not all his benefits . . . so that your youth is renewed like the eagle's" (Psalm 103:2–5).

Personal Exercise #2

III. **The Ultimate Motivation of the Relational Leader: The Opportunity to Love God**
   A. Loving God Through Humility
      1. Like the widow—giving all she had out of humble dependency (Luke 21:1–4)
   B. Loving God Through Faith
      1. Like the Roman Centurion, whose "great faith" amazed Jesus (Luke 7:1-10)
      2. "Without faith it is impossible to please God" (Hebrews 11:6).
   C. Loving God Through Gratitude
      1. Like the Samaritan leper, who could not go one step farther toward Jerusalem without thanking Jesus (Luke 17:11–19)

Experiencing the Word Together #2

My Team Journal

Additional Resources

Leith Anderson, *A Church for the 21st Century* (Minneapolis: Bethany House Publishers, 1992).

Robert K. Greenleaf, *Servant Leadership: A Journey Into the Nature of Legitimate Power and Greatness* (Mahwah, NJ: Paulist Press, 2002).

Denny Gunderson, *The Leadership Paradox* (Dallas: Word Publishing, 1997).

Calvin Miller, *The Empowered Leader: 10 Keys to Servant Leadership* (Nashville: Broadman and Holman, 1997).

Andrew Murray, *Humility* (Springdale, PA: Whitaker House, 1982).

Stacy T. Rinehart, *Upside Down: The Paradox of Servant Leadership* (Colorado Springs: NavPress, 1998).

Bennett J. Sims, *Servanthood: Leadership for the Third Millennium* (Cambridge, MA: Cowley Publications, 1997).

Chapter 3

The Servant's Priority of "Being With" Others

T he Gospels reveal Jesus to be the ultimate relational leader, One who was motivated to humble service by a heart filled with love for His Father and for others (John 10:9–17). Likewise, as relational leaders, we must possess a spirit of servanthood that wells up from a deep love for the heavenly Father, allowing us to overflow with love for other people. Chapter 2 centered on strengthening our "vertical relationship" with the Lord. We emphasized becoming sacrificial servants who express love for God through humble attitudes, faith-filled hearts, and grateful spirits. This chapter will shift the focus to our "horizontal relationships" by exploring ways in which we can prioritize servanthood among those we lead.

Pause now, and reflect on your answers to the following questions:

- Think about a leader who has exhibited a servant's heart, or consider your own perspective of a servant leader. What would this person's actions "look like"? What could you observe about a leader who is characterized by servanthood?

- When have you recently demonstrated an attitude of servanthood? What were some of your specific actions or behaviors that exemplified servanthood?

As you begin to reflect on your "horizontal relationships," consider your commitment to servanthood and how you will live it out. How will you know if you are truly serving the ones God has called you to lead? What priorities should occupy a servant's heart?

"BEING WITH" OTHER PEOPLE
In order to restore the identity of "a people of love" to the 21st century church, we must follow the leadership example of Christ. Jesus led as a servant, humbling Himself and demonstrating the full extent of His love (13:1). He also displayed a unique perspective on relationships and ministry, one which emphasized "being with" others before "doing ministry."

The Example of Jesus

The Gospels point out an important priority for the relational leader. The Scriptures tell us that Jesus went up on the mountainside to pray and then called the disciples whom He wanted (Luke 6:12–16). Mark 3:14 explains that Jesus called the twelve so they might "be with" Him and He might send them out. Let us notice the order of those words. The disciples were first "with Jesus." Then after approximately two years had passed, the Scriptures tell us that He sent them out (Matthew 10:1).

Imagine talking to Peter, James, and John during those first two years of Jesus' ministry. Picture yourself sitting with the disciples at dinner one evening. As you try to get to know these men, you ask the question, "What role do you have in Jesus' ministry?" One of the disciples would eventually give a response such as, "Well, we don't actually have any specific jobs or any definite responsibilities. We're just with Him." Many of us as modern Christian leaders would probably respond incredulously, "What do you mean you are 'just with Him'? What exactly do you do?"

For close to two years the disciples traveled with Jesus as He spoke to the multitudes, taught from the Holy Scriptures, and debated with the Pharisees. They saw Him heal the sick and the lame, watched as He cured the demoniac, and looked on in awe as He brought a young girl back to life. Through all of this, did the disciples "do" anything? No. They were simply with Jesus. But were these two years a waste of time? Would Christ have purposefully let the disciples get by with doing nothing? As strange as it may seem, He **did** allow the disciples to "do nothing" those first two years. He simply wanted to "be with" them.

Jesus was intentional about His plan for the disciples. He gave top priority to "being with" the disciples during those early years, and then implemented the second phase of His plan: He sent them out to minister to others. We even see evidence of this intentional progression as we look at the descriptors for these twelve men. They were first called *disciples* or "learners," and were later given the distinction of *apostles* or "ones who are sent out" (vv. 1, 2).

Just as Jesus deliberately purposed to "be with" the disciples, He also made it a priority to "be with" others. Christ took the time to "be with" the children even when the adults around Him were sure that He was too busy and too important to be bothered by such distractions. Jesus gave priority to "being with" Zacchaeus, suggesting a meal and fellowship rather than reciting a list of ways to make restitution with those he had cheated (Luke 19:1–9).

As Jesus actively modeled "being with" people, He encouraged others to do the same. Mary of Bethany was one who followed His example. Rather than busying herself with "doing things," Mary just wanted to "be with" Jesus, and her actions won the approval of the Savior. "Martha, Martha . . . you are worried and upset about many things, but only one thing is needed. Mary has chosen what is better, and it will not be taken away from her" (10:41). Notice that Mary **chose** the "better thing" by intentionally deciding to "be with" Jesus. The story of Mary and Martha helps us see that "being with" people in an intentional way doesn't come naturally. It must be chosen.

Relational Leaders Prioritize "Being With" Others.

Relational leaders must give priority to "being with" those they lead. Such an approach involves getting to know individuals deeply and intimately just because you care. It requires gaining insight into team members' strengths, weaknesses, hurts, needs, interests, and even failures. It includes spending time with team members in casual and formal settings, church-related activities as well as fun get-togethers. Relational leaders are "with" their teammates when they are

> **"Being with" others involves getting to know them deeply and intimately just because you care.**

vulnerable with personal struggles and honest about their own needs. In every instance, this commitment to "being with" those you lead should precede asking them to "do ministry."

This same priority to "be with" others has its place in the life of the local church as well. Relational leaders can work diligently to provide a "be with" atmosphere for all members of the congregation. Churches can communicate this message to new believers through announcements and procedures that say, "We don't want you to perform any service within our church right now. We don't want to put you to work right away. We just want you to be in our fellowship and enjoy receiving. We want you to first learn to be a good 'receiver' because then and only then can you learn to be a good 'giver' for the cause of Christ" (see Matthew 10:8).

Furthermore, relational leaders can provide a safe place for those who are searching for faith. Churches can communicate a message to those seeking an encounter with Christ that says, "We want to develop a relationship with you rather than attempt to convert you. We want to get to know you rather than try to change you or your beliefs." Relational leaders can work diligently to provide an atmosphere for the "unchurched" that is inviting and non-threatening, yet one in which the message of our Lord is proclaimed boldly.

Overcoming Hindrances to "Being With" Others

What might keep leaders from genuinely "being with" those they lead? The following Personal Exercise will allow us to explore some potential hindrances.

Personal Exercise #1

Brainstorm with at least one other person, and make a list of as many hindrances to "being with" others as you are able to identify.

Some things that might hinder a leader from "being with" other people include . . .

(For example: *preoccupation with my own interests or agenda, uncertainty that anyone would want to spend time just being with me, impatience to accomplish certain tasks, fear of failure if we don't get on with "doing something.")*

Now, look back over your list. You may find that the hindrances you have listed fall into one of three categories: selfishness, self-reliance, or self-condemnation. We have found that leaders are often hindered from "being with" others by their own "issues of self."

- **Selfishness:** Your list undoubtedly contains examples of how leaders may exhibit a "taking thought of me" attitude rather than one that takes thought of others (see Philippians 2:3). This type of leader finds it difficult to "be with" others because he or she is more concerned with meeting his or her own needs and desires.

- **Self-Reliance:** Your list of hindrances may include "self-reliant" hindrances. Self-reliant leaders find it difficult to "be with" those around them because they are not convinced that they need other people, nor that others should need anything from them. A self-reliant leader invariably feels the need to accomplish things in order to feel significant or gain approval, and often comes to view the task as more important than the people.

- **Self-Condemnation:** Finally, your list of hindrances may include hindrances of self-condemnation. The self-condemning leader finds it difficult to "be with" others because he or she is not certain of his or her own personal worth, significance, or value. This type of person may feel that their own worth is so dependent upon "doing something" that simply "being with" people is a waste of time, or that others would not benefit from "being with" them.

Think now about your own ability or inability to "be with" other people and how you might be hindered from making this a priority of leadership. Which of these tendencies best describes you?

I sometimes place my own priorities ahead of my care for others (selfishness).
I can sometimes be more "task focused" than "people focused" (self-reliance).
I can't see why others would value "being with" me (self-condemnation).

I think I might be hindered by my _____ (*selfishness, self-reliance,* or *self-condemnation*) *because I can see that . . .*

For example:

I think I might be hindered by my selfishness because I can see that I struggle with wanting to "check things off my list" and can get irritated if other people sidetrack my efforts.

I think I might be hindered by my self-reliance because I can see that I sometimes just do things myself because I know I'll like the way the job gets done. It seems like too much of an inconvenience to get help with certain projects.

I think I might be hindered by my self-condemnation because I can see that I struggle to believe that others want to spend time with me as much as I desperately want to spend time with them. There are many occasions when I stay busy so that I don't have to risk possible rejection from other people.

You may want to record these responses in the Team Journal at the end of the chapter.

What will it take to overcome these hindrances in you? What will it take to leave behind your issues of self and take thought of others?

Relational leaders understand that the only thing that empowers such a change of heart is the constraining love of Christ (2 Corinthians 5:14 KJV). We will discover more about the love that changes and constrains us throughout the rest of this chapter.

WHY "BEING WITH" OTHERS IS SO IMPORTANT

Perhaps you have entertained some of these thoughts: *Wouldn't we waste a lot of time by trying to "be with" people? We certainly wouldn't get much done. After all, what's wrong with the prevailing approaches to leadership, the ones that encourage casting a vision for what needs to be done and then working hard to influence others to accomplish that vision? Why is it so important to "be with" people?*

To fully grasp the importance of "being with" people, we must imagine being empowered by the same motivation as the apostle Paul. What was it that enabled him to minister to the churches of Corinth, Galatia, and Ephesus? How was he able to "be with" those believers in the early church? Similarly, imagine finding the secret to Christ's mission and leadership. What insight did Christ have that empowered Him to "be with" the disciples?

"Being with" others is important because it is consistent with the loving heart of God. In fact, "being with" others is possible only **because of** the constraining love of God. A servant leader has an experiential understanding of God's loving, compassionate heart for us and those we lead. It is God's love that empowers the leader to think of others and provide for their needs. It is God's love that enables the leader to "be with" others and guard his or her heart from issues of the self. It is God's constraining love that rearranges our priorities.

"Being With" Reflects God's Loving Concern for People's Aloneness.

We see God's first demonstration of His compassionate heart revealed in the first human crisis. He identified a crucial need for every human and then created a divine plan to meet that need. If you were asked to locate the first human crisis, you would surely turn to the early chapters of Genesis. But this first crisis is not found in Genesis 3 with man's fall into sin. It is not the first murder recorded in Genesis 4. The first human crisis is actually recorded in Genesis 2 when the Creator looks at Adam and says, "Adam, it is not good"—not good that he should be alone (Genesis 2:18).

It is important to remember Adam's situation in the Garden. He already had a relationship with God. In fact, Adam had a **perfect** relationship with God. Before the fall of man, there was no sin. Yet God looked at Adam and announced that something was not good. What could possibly have been "not good" about being in paradise, being in charge of paradise, and being in perfect relationship with God while in paradise? Simply put, Adam was alone.

Apparently, Adam needed both a relationship with God and with another human. A sovereign God, free to create us any way He wanted, chose to create us to need both a relationship with Him and relationships with one another. We require both in order to experience the fullness of abundant life (John 10:10). After declaring Adam's aloneness, God ordained relationships. He created marriage, then families, and finally the church (Genesis 2:24; 4:1; Psalm 127:3; Matthew 16:18). Each of these relationships has many God-ordained purposes, but one critical purpose is common to all of them. They were all created by God to remove aloneness.

> **"Being with" others ministers to their aloneness.**

This is a critical idea for us to grasp: it is relationships that remove aloneness—not facts, logic, or reasoning; not what we acquire, accomplish, or achieve; not even knowledge of or proximity to a great number of people. Only intimate relationships with God and one another—relationships that are ordained by Him and empowered by His love—will remove aloneness. As God's love flows through the body of Christ, through our marriages, through our families, aloneness disappears.

It thus becomes clear that the answer to the question, "Why is it so important to 'be with' other people?" is that "being with" others ministers to the "not good" of aloneness in the human heart. As we strive to become servant leaders and "be with" those we are called to lead, God allows us to minister to the lives of people by meeting them at the point of this first human crisis and overcoming their aloneness with His love.

What About Sin?

With all this focus on "being with" and removing aloneness, some may wonder if we are overlooking sin. Shouldn't we be concerned about sin in our lives and in the lives of others?

Yes, absolutely. We *should* be concerned about sin. After all, sin is what keeps us alone, separated from God and other people. Isn't it possible that God sent Jesus to die in part because He did not want sin to isolate us from Him and from one another?

God revealed His deep desire for an intimate relationship with us when He "made Him who had no sin to be sin for us, so that in Him we might become the righteousness of God" (2 Corinthians 5:21). This passage reminds us of the Gospel story. It reveals that Christ took our sin upon Himself and endured the punishment we deserved so that we would not be destined for an eternity of aloneness and separation from God, but rather given acceptance and right standing before God, all because of the gift of divine grace. Our becoming the "righteousness of God" speaks of how much the Father cherishes and desires a relationship with us.

Servant leaders have a deep understanding of this dual purpose of Calvary. They recognize that God provided for our aloneness at Calvary as well as our sin. Out of gratefulness for this provision, relational leaders sense a calling to remove aloneness in others, rather than just talking about sin. They live out the calling: "I want to be a servant leader because it is not good for people to be alone." They have a passionate concern about sin because it offends a holy God **and** because it produces aloneness. Relational leaders may often encounter the "not good" of people's pain and sin, only to be called to love them at the point of their aloneness.

Personal Exercise #2

Pause now, and think about some of the people who have "been with" you at critical moments of your life. Consider some of these questions:

Who was "with" you as you came to Christ? Think about not only those who were physically present, but those who loved you, spent time with you, got to know you, or invested in you as you came to a personal relationship with Christ.

Has there been a particular person or group of people that have "been with" you during times of failure? Did someone "stick with you" even though they knew about your struggles and personal challenges?

Has there been a particular person or group of people that have "been with" you during times of personal crisis? Has someone come alongside you and helped you carry a burden? Did someone help ease your pain with their supportive care?

Now, as you reflect on one or more of these relationships, consider this: how were you less alone because of this person "being with" you?

As I reflect on how this person was "with me," I realize that it was so meaningful to me because I was less alone in that . . .

Share this with one or more group members, as instructed by your leader. You may want to record these responses in the Team Journal at the end of the chapter.

Just as we reflected on the blessing that occurs when leaders give priority to "being with" those they lead, we must also look at the pain that can occur when leaders do not focus on relationships. How can we know if we, as leaders, are not prioritizing "being with" other people?

SYMPTOMS OF NOT "BEING WITH"

As we look closely at today's leaders, there are several glaring indicators of not "being with" those we lead. One indicator is a focus on the temporal rather than the eternal. Some leaders prioritize temporal concerns with getting things done and accomplishing more, rather than eternal issues such as God, His Word, and other people. A second indicator is a focus on comparison and competition rather than service and unity. This type of leader strives to win and get ahead, often at the expense of those they are supposed to serve. Finally, a third potential indicator is a focus on autonomy and self-righteousness rather than interdependence and love. These leaders often breed division and dissension among those they lead.

Let us take a closer look at these symptoms of not "being with" others.

A Focus on the Temporal Instead of the Eternal

Picture yourself at the monthly pastor's meeting. Ministers are gathered together to pray for their city and support one another. Pastor Al and his wife Jan attend the meeting because of their burden for the community and the opportunity to come together with others who share a similar heart. During the meeting, the pastors discuss the details for organizing an annual "Day of Prayer" and then have lunch together. Al and Jan enjoy visiting with two other ministry couples at their table. When asked how their ministry is going, Al relates the blessing of seeing their congregation demonstrate care for one another as well as some of the challenges of ministry. "It has been fantastic to sense that our people have a genuine concern for one another, and that concern has been contagious. We've seen lives changed within our church and gained a fresh perspective on evangelism. God has never shown Himself like this before. Seeing Him move in such great ways has helped offset the pain that Jan and I feel over one particular couple. I'm sure you've been there, too. We poured our lives into this couple, and they have continued to struggle personally, as well as negatively impact others in our church. It's been painful to watch, and we don't always know how to respond."

As the next pastor shares about his ministry, the focus is quite different. "We're celebrating our tenth anniversary at the church this year, and God has been so good. We've built three buildings and relocated our Christian school. We sure have learned a lot. You never know what objections those neighborhood associations will think of next." Another leader gives an update on her church. "God has been doing tremendous things among us, too. We've exceeded the budget in tithes for the last six months, and our missions budget is about to expand as well."

As we imagine that meeting of local pastors, we must ask ourselves, "Isn't ministry more than budgets and buildings? Isn't God interested in more than increasing the numbers and achieving the financial goals?" God must be grieved when His leaders focus on the temporal instead of the eternal. Christ felt the same painful burden as He encountered leaders whose focus was upon the physical rather than the spiritual. Consider the account of the Transfiguration. Christ went to the mountain, accompanied by Peter, James, and John, the closest of His disciples. The Bible tells us that Jesus began to talk with Moses and Elijah. Then the heavenly Father looked down from heaven and announced, "This is my Son, whom I love; with him I am well pleased. Listen to him!" (Matthew 17:5). Christ fellowshipped with the transfigured spirits of the Old Testament, and Jehovah Himself spoke words of praise and commendation within the disciples' hearing. Yet what was their response? "Rabbi, it is good for us to be here. Let us put up three shelters—one for you, one for Moses and one for Elijah. (He did not know what to say, they were so frightened)" (Mark 9:5, 6). Rather than focus upon the miraculous spiritual event they had just witnessed, the disciples focused on the physical and suggested putting up tabernacles! Their minds were preoccupied with the temporal and missed the majesty of the eternal.

A Focus on Competition and Comparison Instead of Unity and Servanthood

Larry and Sharon attend quarterly meetings for adult Bible study teachers. They dread these meetings but aren't exactly sure why they have concerns. Some fellow teachers take the opportunity to check on the status of each class: "How many are you running on Sunday? We've doubled our attendance from last year. How about you?" Other teachers seem to use these meetings as an opportunity to air frustrations or complain about the challenges of ministry. "We just can't seem to hit our attendance goals. The couples in our class have little kids, and that means they're out sick or sleep in. We can't count on any of them." Finally, there is also a group of teachers that seems to measure their success by those around them. Their comments are always made with a lighthearted tone, but they produce an environment of competition: "Our breakfast for High-Attendance Day sure was a success! We had to bring in extra chairs from Joe's class just to seat everybody. The room was packed full!"

Christ's heart must have been grieved when His own disciples' focus on status and achievement turned into competition and comparison. The Gospel of Matthew tells us of a mother's request, two disciples' petition, and the conflict that resulted. James and John entered a house in Jerusalem along with their mother. She knelt before Jesus and asked Him to give preferential treatment to her sons, saying "Grant that one of these two sons of mine may sit at your right and the other at your left in your kingdom" (Matthew 20:21). The other ten disciples were indignant when they heard about James and John's request. These two men focused upon competition instead of servanthood, and the result was disharmony within the group.

A Focus on Autonomy and Self-righteousness Instead of Interdependence and Love

Janna loves to talk about the Lord's ministry through *Rebecca's House*. One of her favorite things to do is to travel to churches in her area to tell others about how the Lord has worked in her life and the lives of the women that come to the ministry. This particular night she is speaking at First Church of Atlanta. Janna tells the audience that many of the women are receptive to the Gospel because of the crises surrounding their unwed pregnancy. She also explains that her team makes it a priority to get to know each woman and build relationships, as well as sharing their faith in Christ (1 Thessalonians 2:7, 8).

As Janna takes questions from the audience, one of the church leaders raises his hand to speak. "Don't you think it's important to talk with these girls about what got them there in the first place? Sooner or later, they need to learn from their mistakes." Janna is ready for his question and gives a gentle yet redirective response. "Yes, I do think it is important for these young women to learn from their mistakes. At the same time, we work hard to respond to these women like Christ responded to the woman caught in adultery. His first priority was to 'be with' her, kneeling on the ground, entering her world, and demonstrating care. Then, second, Jesus addressed the woman's sin (John 8:3–8). We have all made mistakes and endured the consequences for our sin. At *Rebecca's House*, we realize that we not only need to confess that sin and make it right with God, we often need someone to 'be with' us as we deal with the pain that comes as a result of sin."

Next, a female leader on the front row inquires about how their church could best support *Rebecca's House*. Janna explains that donations of baby and maternity items are always needed, but even more important are the emotional and spiritual needs of the young ladies. Janna gives details about the vast number of volunteers that are needed just to "be with" the unwed mothers. She describes how they need people who will listen to each woman's story and show supportive care.

This same female leader smiles with enthusiasm and says, "I think what these women need most is to find employment. If they could find jobs, then they might be able to 'better themselves,' and stay out of trouble in the process." Janna agreed with part of this observation. "You are right. Many of our women do need to find a job, and we try to help them face the financial challenges of providing for their babies. But we have also discovered that everyone needs help 'carrying their burdens' from time to time. So at *Rebecca's House,* we try to live out Galatians 6:2. We try to help the women bear the burdens that come with an unwed pregnancy."

Jesus must feel a sense of sorrow when He hears church leaders giving priority to their own agendas and autonomous concerns. He must weep when He hears church leaders' self-righteous accusations. By contrast, Christ sees His body, the church, as one connected whole. He sees the suffering of one member and understands how it affects the entire church. He sees the pain of one part of the body and knows how it will hurt another. Jesus wants the leadership of His church to focus upon creating an environment of humility and mutual dependency so that each part of the body will have "equal concern for one another" (1 Corinthians 12:24–26).

Now that we have explored some signs of not "being with" those we lead, let us return to our consideration of what it means to be a servant and give priority to relationships.

"BEING WITH" REQUIRES "GIVING FIRST."

Servant leaders are to live like Christ and "be with" those they lead. "Being with" others is synonymous with "giving first." When we place priority on "being with" people, we are giving of ourselves and "giving first," without expecting anything in return. When we are with others, and giving to them first, we live out Christ's command in Luke 6:38: "Give, and it will be given to you," and model our actions after the heart of God in John 3:16: "For God so loved the world that He **gave**. . . ."

Jesus "Gave First."

Christ demonstrated this heart of "giving first" as He ministered to the multitudes. Mark 8:1–3 reveals the sensitivity of the Savior to the needs of people. Jesus had been teaching the crowds near the Sea of Galilee, and the Scriptures tell us that He was moved with compassion because of their needs. He called his disciples to Him and said, "I have compassion for these people; they have already been with me three days and have nothing to eat. If I send them home hungry, they will collapse on the way, because some of them have come a long distance" (vv. 2, 3). Jesus, the Son of God, was deeply impacted by the crowd's hunger and was keenly sensitive to their life situation. He took initiative to meet their physical needs and provided abundantly. No one asked Jesus to do this. He simply gave, and "gave first!"

Jesus also demonstrated a heart that "gives first" when He ministered to individuals. The Savior "gave first" to the woman at the well by initiating contact with her in spite of the facts that she was a Samaritan and a female, and He clearly went out of His way to give her the opportunity to receive eternal life (John 4:7–39). Jesus also "gave first" to the man born blind. John 9:1–41 gives an account of Christ's extravagant giving on this man's behalf. Jesus gave him sight even though there was no request or plea for healing. Christ simply saw the need and provided abundantly. The Scriptures further illustrate the Savior's giving heart by telling us that Jesus went out of His way to encounter the man a second time. Because of His heart of compassion, Christ wanted to find the man and demonstrate care when He heard that the church leaders had "put him out" of the synagogue.

Finally, the Savior demonstrated a heart that "gives first" when He provided for **us**. Jesus left His world of glory to enter our world of sin and pain. He sacrificially gave up His home in heaven so that He could come to earth and die a horrific death in order to provide eternal life for you and me. Romans 5:8 tells us that Christ gave up His life for us even while we were sinners, and Ephesians 5:2 explains that "Christ loved us and gave himself up for us as a fragrant offering and sacrifice to God."

How Can We "Give First"?

Since Jesus loved us and gave Himself first for us, we must ask ourselves how we can "give first" to others in like manner. We "give first" when we are sensitive to the needs and life situations of those around us and take initiative to meet those needs. This type of "giving first" might involve being sensitive to the life stress that comes with the birth of a baby and offering to run errands for the new mother. Leaders also "give first" when they go out of their way to provide for those they are called to serve. This might entail making a special effort to establish a relationship with the teenage son of a single mom by inviting the young man to play golf, attending his basketball games, or taking interest in his academics. Finally, "giving first" often means giving with a sacrificial love. For instance, a church leader might privately give a monetary donation so that church members could attend the annual retreat without financial burden. Perhaps a minister or church leader could "give first" by being the first one to volunteer for church-wide work days, neighborhood outreach events, or building fund campaigns. In all these ways, servant leaders "give first," just as Christ "gave first" to us.

Once again, we must ask the question: how will we sustain this servant heart that gives priority to "being with" others and "giving first"? It will not be sustained by acquiring more knowledge or through sheer determination. What will empower our "being with" and "giving first"?

Where Does Our Ability to "Give First" Come From?

The Book of Ephesians gives us insight into the power that will sustain the servant's ministry. "Be imitators of God, therefore, as dearly loved children and live a life of love" (5:1, 2). If we are not careful, we may miss the keys that unlock the power to live this life of love. The apostle Paul tells the church at Ephesus to be imitators of God, as "dearly loved children." These words reveal the power that will sustain and motivate our life of "giving first" and "being with" others: it is only from an experience of being dearly loved by God that we can deeply love others. Our gratefulness for how we have been loved, for how Christ has "been with" us and "given first" to us, will empower our "giving first" to others.

> **Gratefulness for the ways in which God has "given first" to us will empower us to "give first" to others.**

Consider how Christ has loved you dearly, how He has "given first" to you. Perhaps He "gave first" by providing for a financial need in an unexpected way, or by blessing you with a cherished marriage partner. Christ may have "given first" by bringing sustaining grace in the midst of a trial or perfect peace in the middle of life's storms. Reflect on the previous exercise in this chapter that dealt with your gratefulness for the blessing of someone "being with" you. Could it be that Christ was actually loving you, and "being with" you through that special person? Could it be that it was actually Jesus "giving first"?

How is your heart affected when you consider how Christ has "given first" to you? Does the thought prompt gratitude? Humility? Love? Recognition of the love that we received first from Him is what will empower our love for others.

Experiencing the Word Together

"Thanks be to God for his indescribable gift" (2 Corinthians 9:15)!

Take a moment and reflect on this One whose very nature is to "be with" and "give first." He is determined to "be with" us despite our selfishness, our prideful self-reliance, or our self-condemnation. He "gives first" in the face of our competition, comparisons, and division. God "gives first" even in the midst of our sin. His heart is described well in the story of the prodigal son (Luke 15:11–32).

Imagine the scene: a son approaches his father one day, demanding his inheritance and demanding it early. The son selfishly says to his father, "Give to me what is mine." The son then takes that which is his and squanders it. Before long, the son has spent all he has and finds himself in need.

In his self-reliance, the son says, "I know what will take care of this. I will work for this pig farmer. I got myself into this. I'll get myself out." You can almost hear the prideful ambition in his voice. "I'll handle it. I can do it alone." Yet the son finds himself unable to escape his problems. He stoops so low as to eat the pigs' food, and begins to imagine that the servants of his father must eat much better than he.

The son now begins to question his own worth to his father. His self-condemnation keeps him in the pig sty, feeling too insignificant and ashamed to return to his father's house. He struggles with the decision to go back home, but as he imagines the father's care for his servants, God uses that to stir his heart. So the son begins to make his way back to his father.

Can you imagine the anxiety that must have flooded his heart and the doubts that filled his mind? "What will my father's reaction be? What kind of punishment is in store? How many countless questions will I have to answer? How many lectures will I have to endure?" Picture the scene: the son makes his way home with all of those fears, all of those doubts, all of those questions weighing him down. And he makes that final turn toward home.

Now, imagine that you are the son or daughter who has selfishly demanded what is yours. Imagine that you are that prodigal who has foolishly proclaimed your self-reliance. Imagine that you are that child who questions your very worth, unsure of your significance and too ashamed to face your father. Now it is you who makes that final turn toward home. The Gospel of Luke says, "While he was still a long way off, his father saw him and was filled with compassion for him; he ran to his son, threw his arms around him and kissed him" (15:20). Picture this same scene in your heart: your Father sees you a long way off, His heart is moved with compassion, and He comes running off that front porch toward you. Not with lectures, not with condemnation, not with criticism, but to embrace you with loving arms. Your Father rushes up to you, and kisses you again and again. He puts a robe around you, bestows a ring of favor, and gives instructions to begin a party in your honor.

What do you feel as you consider your Father's response to you? How is your heart stirred by the knowledge of God's longing to be with you? How are you affected as you sense that the Father has been waiting for you, desperately wanting to love you and give to you?

Express your gratitude for the Father's heart that "gives first" despite your selfishness, self-reliance, or self-condemnation.

Heavenly Father, I am grateful for Your heart of love, a love that gives first . . .
I am overwhelmed by feelings of . . .
I want the love that I have received from You to empower my love for . . .

Take the time to pray privately, and then share your prayerful responses with one or more group members as directed by your facilitator. You may want to record these responses in the Team Journal at the end of the chapter.

Relational leaders begin their pursuit of servanthood by first experiencing the love of Jesus and by recalling and reflecting on all the ways that Christ has loved us. As we experience His love, we are compelled to demonstrate our love for Him and it is out of that love relationship that we are empowered to love others.

Don't ever miss the glory of the fact that you have been and are loved. Don't ever lose sight of the marvelous, unconditional, constraining love that will empower you to demonstrate the heart of a servant toward others.

My Team Journal

■ What might keep leaders from being able to "be with" those they lead? Record your list of ideas here:

_____

_____

_____

_____

■ Which of the three hindrances (selfishness, self-reliance, self-condemnation) did each group member identify?

Name: Responses:

_____

_____

_____

_____

■ How did each group member respond to the question, Who has "been with" you at critical moments of your life?

Name: Responses:

_____

_____

_____

_____

■ How did each person respond to the meditation of the loving Father? What feelings were prompted? What prayers were offered?

Name: Responses:

_____

_____

_____

_____

_____

■ How might God want you to prioritize "being with" each member of your team? How might God want you to "give first" to the members of your team?

Name: Ways I can "be with" and "give first" to them:

_____

_____

_____

_____

_____

Chapter 3 Outline

I. "Being With" Other People

  A. The Example of Jesus

    1. "He appointed twelve . . . that they might be with Him" (Mark 3:14).

    2. "Being with" them for close to two years preceded sending them out.

    3. He also prioritized "being with" all kinds of people: children, the Samaritan woman at the well, Mary, Martha, Lazarus, and Zacchaeus.

  B. Relational Leaders Prioritize "Being With" Others.

    1. Getting to know others because we care (How might we do this?)

    2. Letting others know us, including our needs and struggles

    3. Communicating a message to new people in the church or ministry: "We want to know you and let you know us before we ask you to do anything!"

    4. Communicating to those who haven't yet come to faith: "We want to have a relationship with you rather than only attempting to convert you."

  C. Overcoming Hindrances to "Being With" Others

    1. Selfishness: "I'm more concerned about me than I am about 'being with' you."

    2. Self-reliance: "I'm not sure I need to 'be with' you."

    3. Self-condemnation: "I'm not sure I'm worth 'being with.'"

  Personal Exercise #1

II. Why "Being With" Others Is So Important

  A. "Being With" Reflects God's Loving Concern for People's Aloneness.

    1. He declared, "It is not good . . . to be alone" (Genesis 2:18).

    2. He then provided the solution: human relationships that remove aloneness.

    3. Our "being with" others helps remove their aloneness.

B. What About Sin?

    1. We should be concerned about sin—sin is what keeps us alone!

        a. Sin separates us from God.

        b. Sin separates us from each other.

    2. The dual purpose of the Cross: God's provision for both sin and aloneness

    3. Relational leaders express concern for sin out of a calling to remove aloneness.

Personal Exercise #2

III. Symptoms of Not "Being With"

A. A Focus on the Temporal Instead of the Eternal

    1. Temporal: Budgets, buildings, and "measurables"

    2. At the transfiguration of Jesus, the disciples wanted to build shelters instead of listening to (being with) Jesus (Mark 9:2–8).

B. A Focus on Competition and Comparison Instead of Unity and Servanthood

    1. "How many are you running? We've doubled our attendance!"

    2. James and John asked for the best places in the Kingdom; the other disciples became indignant (Matthew 20:20–24).

C. A Focus on Autonomy and Self-Righteousness Instead of Interdependence and Love

    1. Encouraging independent "take-care-of-yourself" personal responsibility apart from compassionate and appropriate "bearing of burdens"

    2. Focusing on "who's to blame" rather than on how we can solve the problem together

    3. What's needed: the church as the body of Christ having "equal concern for each other" (1 Corinthians 12:25)

IV. "Being With" Requires "Giving First."

A. Jesus Gave First.

    1. He realized that the multitudes were hungry, so He initiated feeding them (Mark 8:1–10).

    2. He initiated contact with the Samaritan woman at the well, going out of His way to encounter her and talk with her (John 4:4–38).

    3. He initiated healing the man born blind, then went looking for him when He heard that the man had been put out of the synagogue (9:1–41).

    4. He left His world of glory to enter our world of sin and pain, and died in order to give us eternal life (3:16).

B. How Can We "Give First"?

    1. Meeting needs: giving support to a family with a new baby, establishing relationships with single-parent children

    2. Doing first what we encourage others to do: anonymous financial giving, initiating getting to know others, being real with others about our struggles

C. Where Does Our Ability to "Give First" Come From?

    1. Gratefulness for how God has "been with" us

    2. Gratefulness for how God has "given first" to us

Experiencing the Word Together

My Team Journal

Additional Resources

Max Lucado, *A Love Worth Giving* (Thomas Nelson, Nashville, 2002).

Charles C. Manz, *The Leadership Wisdom of Jesus* (San Francisco: Berrett-Koehler Publishers, 1998).

Henri J. M. Nouwen, *In the Name of Jesus: Reflections on Christian Leadership* (New York: Crossroad Publishing, 1989).

Alan Redpath, *The Making of a Man of God* (Old Tappan, NJ: Fleming H. Revell Company, 1962).

Chapter 4

The Experience of Fellowship: A Caring Team Sharing Christ's Love

(9:00 on a Monday morning. A conversation is taking place between Janna, the facilitator of Rebecca's House, *a crisis pregnancy center, and Marcia, a teen volunteer at the center. The two are in Janna's office.)*

MARCIA:
Janna, I just don't get this relational leadership stuff. You've asked me to help out at the center, but you've also told me I'm not supposed to try to be a leader. Instead, I'm supposed to be like Jesus. That's way out of my league!

JANNA:
Marcia, slow down for a moment. I know it sounds like a big stretch to aspire to Christlike leadership, but stop and consider how He led and how He encouraged others. Jesus didn't just pop down to earth and demand that the disciples start doing ministry. According to Mark 3, He called His disciples to "be with" Him. He got to know them, lived with them, and loved them for two years. Think about it. Have you ever wondered what Jesus, a carpenter, was doing down at the lake? He was there to enter the world of fishermen like Peter, Andrew, James, and John. And why do you think He hung around the tax office? It was because of tax collectors like Matthew. So when I encourage you and the rest of the team to lead like Jesus, I'm first encouraging you to "be with" the ladies who come here. I'm encouraging you to enter their world.

MARCIA:
Yeah, but Jesus was **God**. He performed miracles and was a wise teacher. It's no wonder Jesus was a great leader. He did big stuff!

JANNA:
Sure, He did "big stuff," but He also cared about the "little stuff" in the lives of those He served. Remember when He was in Capernaum, and went to Peter's house? He discovered that

Peter's mother-in-law had a fever. Jesus touched her hand, and she was cured. But as important as it was that Jesus performed a miracle that day, it was just as significant that He showed concern for Peter. Christ knew the things that were going on in Peter's life and cared about what was important to him. So I'm challenging our team to do the same. When these ladies come to the center, we need to learn about the pain they've experienced and show them we care. We need to know about the things that brought them here and discover what's important to them. We must care about the "stuff" in their lives.

MARCIA:
So leadership means getting to know these women and even sharing their pain? It seems like that would take a long time. Besides, their personal lives aren't really any of my business.

JANNA:
Marcia, as I have come to know you, I've been saddened by the painful experiences that originally brought you to *Rebecca's House*. If you stop and examine your feelings, I think you'll realize that it's out of gratitude for God's care for your pain that you volunteer and care for these women. You've felt the same kind of loneliness and heartache that many of our ladies experience, and that gives you great compassion for them.

MARCIA:
(With tears in her eyes) I am very grateful for God's love and the acceptance He's shown me through you and others. I do sympathize with what these women are going through, and I do hurt for them. But what if they don't want to share with me? They might think I won't understand.

JANNA:
When you tell them your own story, they'll know you care, Marcia. Your openness will help these ladies not feel so alone. After all, that's how Jesus led. You know the passage where Jesus tells us that He's the "Good Shepherd." He says, "I know my sheep and my sheep know me" (John 10:14). Those are two of the fundamental ways we care for people: we come to know them and let them know us. I'm confident you can love people like that.

MARCIA:
Being honest about my past is hard for me, but if it will help someone else, then I'm willing to try. But I don't think I can do it without your support.

JANNA:

Don't worry. I will walk with you through the process. It will be a growing experience for both of us. Remember, we're a team!

Building a caring and connected team is a critical step in living out our call to be servant leaders. Indeed, without the presence of such a team, "relational leadership" quickly ceases to be relational. Coming together as a team allows us to intentionally care for one another and, in turn, to serve others well. As relational leaders, we must seek to promote the pursuit of both of these goals. We must first foster a sense of unity and mutual care among our team that supercedes individual agendas, and then encourage the group to place a higher priority on touching people than on "achieving objectives."

> **Relational leaders must build a caring and connected team.**

The preceding dialogue between Janna and Marcia portrays a leader who has fully embraced this philosophy. Janna patiently listens to Marcia's concerns, expresses care for her, challenges her to extend love and compassion to the women at the center, and pledges to walk alongside her as they meet future challenges together. These are all essential elements of a relational approach to teambuilding.

As we strive to build caring and connected teams in this way, we will undoubtedly face significant challenges. Sadly, our most formidable obstacles may arise from within the church itself, as it seems that the Western church now tends to prioritize "getting things done" over knowing and caring for people. This is a dangerous departure from the approach of the New Testament church. In Acts 2:42, Luke observed these attributes of the early Christians: "They devoted themselves to the apostles' teaching and to the fellowship, to the breaking of bread and to prayer."

Now, consider the church of the 21st century. Do we experience all four of these elements of worship that were practiced among the early believers? Reflect on your most recent church experience. Was the Word of God preached? Undoubtedly. Did you pray together with other Christians? Of course. Was communion observed (or, depending on your tradition, will it be duly observed in the near future)? Almost assuredly. But now a very important question must be asked: Did you experience genuine fellowship (*koinonia*)? Did you come to more intimately know another part of His body, or did everyone focus only on activities and responsibilities? Was priority given to creating a safe place where God's people could be real with one another, or was there pressure to wear masks of self-protection? Was the Spirit allowed to lead people into intentional and genuine care for one another? If we define true fellowship in this way, most of us would have to voice a resounding "no" to the *koinonia* question. And tragically, many of us would have to admit that we have apparently missed this special fellowship with other believers without even realizing it.

The purpose of this chapter and the following one is to explore some key elements of genuine fellowship and caring connectedness. Chapters 6 and 7 will then address another aspect of *koinonia*, namely "partnering for a purpose." Throughout this chapter we will have the opportunity to experience true fellowship and to take the first steps toward building our own caring teams that will share God's love.

Personal Exercise #1

Take a moment now to reflect on your own experiences within a team. As you remember your time spent with various ministry, career, or community teams, consider how you would complete the following sentence:

I sense that I am an important part of a team when . . .

(For example: *I sense that I am an important part of a team when others keep me updated on their contributions and responsibilities and they, in turn, want to know about mine.*)

Share your responses with one or two participants as directed by your facilitator.

As you have focused on what it means to be a valuable, important part of a team, you may have concluded that your previous leaders must have done some things well. They must have had a sense of what it takes to build a caring, connected team. How do we build that kind of team? We must look again to the leadership of Jesus.

REAFFIRMING THE PRIORITY OF "BEING WITH" BEFORE "SENDING OUT"

"Jesus went up on a mountainside and called to him those he wanted . . . that they might be with him and that he might send them out . . ." (Mark 3:13, 14).

The Disciples' Possible Reactions

Mark 3:14 reveals Christ's technique for building His team of twelve. As previously stated, Jesus gave priority to "being with" His disciples before sending them out to do ministry. Can you picture the conversation that this approach might have generated? The disciples must have been ready to "go and do something." Peter may have wanted to start a ministry to fishermen. Perhaps Matthew felt compelled to create a new support group for tax collectors. As you imagine the ideas that were exchanged and the brainstorming that took place, visualize the Savior's response. Jesus might have assured them that they **would** get around to doing those kinds of things eventually, but He undoubtedly reemphasized the importance of first getting to know and caring for one another.

Personal Exercise #2

Put yourself in the place of the disciples. It is the day after your calling to become one of Christ's followers. What would you be ready to do? Would you respond like Peter? Peter was often impulsive, impatient, and even prideful. If you are impulsive like Peter, you might launch the first program that came to mind. You might be the kind of person who wants to "do something" even if it is wrong! Or would you instead respond like Philip? You might lay out a very rational and strategic plan for how to accomplish the tasks at hand. Like Philip, you might be very focused on the "how to's" and the practical side of life. Perhaps, like James and John, your competitive nature would emerge. You might be preoccupied with the pride that comes with knowing that you have been chosen as a part of the "few" rather than grouped with the masses.

Think about each of the disciples and their unique characteristics. Which of the disciples sounds most like you? Now, complete the following sentence:

I can see myself being like_____(Peter)_____ (or Philip, or James and John) because . . .

For example:

I can see myself being a little like Peter because I definitely have an impulsive side. When there's a job to be done, I am the first one to "jump in." I may not have a plan, but there's plenty of action.

I can see myself being a little like Philip because I tend to sit back and analyze the situation before taking any action. I like to think through all the scenarios and make a detailed plan before I implement any ideas.

I can see myself being a little like James and John. I do like to compare how I'm doing with everyone else and how I'm measuring up.

Share your responses with one or two other members as directed by your facilitator.

Jesus' Care for the Disciples' Concerns

Now that you have had the opportunity to identify with one of the disciples, take a moment and reflect specifically on Peter's experience with the Lord. He was called to be one of the twelve disciples, and for almost two years he spent time just "being with" Jesus. Imagine the surprise that Peter must have felt the day he heard Christ's announcement: "We're going to your house to care for your mother-in-law." What was it that moved Christ's heart to go to Capernaum and heal her? Did simple concern for an elderly woman prompt Christ's actions? Most certainly. Did He possess an abiding sympathy for the sick and hurting? Of course. Did He desire to bring His Father glory? Absolutely. But Christ was also moved with compassion for the pain that Peter must have felt because someone he loved was ill. Jesus had come to know Peter and the concerns of his heart, and their relationship provided part of the motivation for the Savior's loving response. Imagine how Peter must have felt as He traveled to Capernaum, knowing that his burdens were on Christ's heart.

Jesus' Care for Our Concerns

The wondrous truth is that Jesus cares for you just as He did for Peter. His first priority is not to get you to do a certain job or accomplish a specific task, but simply to "be with" you. And as He is with you, Jesus wants to demonstrate compassion for the burdens of your heart. He wants you to know that He cares for you specifically, individually, and unconditionally.

What if it were true that you were more to Him than someone He wanted to use? What if Jesus wanted to know about your life, your cares, and your burdens? What if He truly cared about the "small stuff" in your world? Imagine Him saying, "We're going to your house to care for your burdens. I want to come with you because I care deeply about your financial stress, family conflict, aging parents, or sick child."

The Savior **does** care that much for you. Your burdens move Him with compassion and prompt His intervention on your behalf. That kind of loving care should deeply impact our hearts. What does it do to **your** heart to know that you have a Savior who knows you and is concerned about the anxieties of your life?

Experiencing the Word Together #1

"Cast all your anxiety on him because he cares for you" (1 Peter 5:7).

Consider a burden on your heart, and share intimately with Jesus.

I am reminded of this burden: _____.

(For example: *I am reminded of the financial pressures I am facing.* Or *I am reminded of my daughter who is out of God's will.*)

Pause now, and share your burden with Jesus. Express your hurts to the Lord and then allow His Spirit to speak words of care and comfort to your heart.

Dear Jesus, I have this burden on my heart and I need to be reassured that you care. . . .

Imagine Christ sharing with you like He did with Peter: "I want to share in this hardship with you. I am here for you. Give those cares and burdens to Me. I'll help lighten your load. You can count on Me because I love you."

As you finish praying, share your heart-response with one another. Relate how much it means to you to have a God who cares about your life, your burdens, and your anxieties.

As I reflect on Christ being interested in me and my burdens, my heart is moved with . . . (For example: *awe, gratitude, surprise,* or *amazement*).

Share with a partner or group as directed by your facilitator.

As you have shared your responses to the preceding experiential exercise, you have experienced God's care. Receiving His care is critical if we hope to be able to extend that same kind of care to one another and to the world around us. This is the first step toward building a caring, connected team and restoring the genuine fellowship of the early church.

Having established this foundation, we can now explore further aspects of Christ's teambuilding strategy. Jesus offers three guiding principles as He speaks of His own leadership in John 10:14, 15: "I am the good shepherd; **I know my sheep** and **my sheep know Me** . . . and **I lay down my life for the sheep**."

BUILDING A CARING AND CONNECTED TEAM BY KNOWING THEM

We will now look at the first evidence of a "good shepherd"—a "good shepherd" **knows the sheep**. Christ gave priority to "being with" his team of twelve for their first two years of ministry. But what could Jesus have been doing for those two years? How was He leading His team? Jesus was "being with" the disciples; and through that process, He came to know them. He experienced genuine fellowship with the twelve and just like the "Good Shepherd" of John 10, He developed a confident understanding and deep knowledge of His disciples. But **how** did He develop these things? How did Jesus get to know His team?

> **Building a caring and connected team requires knowing others, letting others know you, and sacrifically caring for others.**

Knowing About Their Important Relationships

First, Jesus came to know those He led by entering their world of **relationships**. Christ demonstrated His specific knowledge of relationships when He was introduced to Simon Peter. As Andrew heard the Messiah's teachings and witnessed John's testimony that Jesus was "the Lamb of God," he brought his own brother to Jesus. The Savior looked at Simon, acknowledged his family relationships, and gave him the name *Peter*: "You are Simon son of John. You will be called Cephas [which is translated Peter]" (John 1:42). On another occasion, Christ entered the world of relationships as He listened to a mother's request. "Then the mother of Zebedee's sons came to Jesus with her sons and, kneeling down, asked a favor of him" (Matthew 20:20). We cannot help but think that Jesus gave audience to this woman's concerns because of His deep knowledge of and genuine love for the men on His team. As previously mentioned, Jesus entered Peter's world of relationships when He showed concern for his mother-in-law. "When

Jesus came into Peter's house, he saw Peter's mother-in-law lying in bed with a fever. He touched her hand and the fever left her . . ." (8:14, 15). Christ came to know His team by developing a deep, empathetic understanding of the relationships that they deemed important.

In this same way, a relational leader will come to know a team by entering their world of relationships. Do you know the name of each of your team members' spouses (if they are married) or close friends (if unmarried)? Have you met each team member's children, and can you call them by name? **Have you developed a depth of understanding and care for the relationships that are important to your team?**

Knowing About Their Activities and Interests

Jesus came to know the people He led by entering their world of **activities and interests**. Jesus, a carpenter by trade, left His world of carpentry and entered the world of fishermen. "As Jesus was walking beside the Sea of Galilee, he saw two brothers, Simon called Peter and his brother Andrew. They were casting a net into the lake, for they were fishermen" (4:18). Christ did not just stumble upon these men or happen by their dock. He had to leave His neighborhood, His world, and go in search of these members of His team. He initiated the communication and showed interest in their activities.

Jesus also entered the disreputable world of a tax collector. "As Jesus went on from there, he saw a man named Matthew sitting at the tax collector's booth" (9:9). The Gospel of Matthew goes on to tell us that Jesus even went to Matthew's house and had dinner with his friends. Jesus came to know Matthew by spending time with him. Christ was willing to enter the world of a tax collector even though it jeopardized His reputation.

A relational leader will want to make it a priority to be a part of the activities and interests of his or her team. How does each member of your team spend most of his or her leisure time? What hobbies do they have? What forms of recreation do they most enjoy? Can you answer these questions? Have you "been with" team members as they are doing things they like to do? **Do you show interest in your team members' activities?**

Knowing About Their Celebrations and Struggles

Jesus came to know the people He led by entering their world of **celebrations**. The Sea of Galilee provided the backdrop for a celebration when Jesus challenged the disciples to let down their nets in the middle of the day: "Master, we've worked hard all night and haven't caught anything," they complained (Luke 5:5). But Luke goes on to tell us that Christ provided so many fish that the boats began to sink. A second, similar celebration occurred when Christ encountered Peter and his companions after another fruitless fishing trip: "They went out and got into the boat, but that night they caught nothing" (John 21:3). Jesus then gave abundant provision and cause for celebration, turning failure into joy: "'Throw your net on the right side of the boat and you will find some.' When they did, they were unable to haul the net in because of the large number of fish" (v. 6).

Likewise, Christ entered the disciples' world of **struggles** with warmth and sensitivity. In John 13:33, Christ revealed His destiny to the disciples. Wanting to prepare the disciples for the events ahead, He spoke of His impending death: "I will be with you only a little longer. . . . Where I am going, you cannot come." As the men began to struggle with this news, Christ comforted their anxiety and fear. "Do not let your heart be troubled; believe in God, believe also in Me. . . . I go to prepare a place for you" (14:1, 2 NASB). Jesus was moved with compassion as He saw the disciples' pain at the announcement of His imminent departure.

Likewise, the relational leader will want to give priority to team members' celebrations and struggles. **Have you been aware of your team's celebrations? Have you truly rejoiced along with them? Have you been aware of your team members' struggles? Have you entered into these struggles with sensitivity and compassion?**

Finally, we must note that in all these things, Jesus was exemplifying the eternal heart of God. The Scriptures not only provide us with ample proof that the Son of God came to know and care for His disciples, they also give evidence of a Father who knows and cares for us. Consider for a moment the Hebrew word *yada*, which means "to know; or an intimate knowledge of another person." Jeremiah spoke of the Lord knowing him: "Before I formed you in the womb I knew you . . ." (Jeremiah 1:5). The Psalmist wrote, "O Lord . . . you know me" (Psalm 139:1). We, too, have a God who knows us, inside and out. He knows our strengths, weaknesses, secrets, failures, and deepest desires. Just as Christ knew of the disciples' relationships, God knows all about the relationships that are closest to our hearts. Just as Jesus left His world and took interest in the disciples' world, we have a God who takes interest in us. And just as the Son came to know the disciples through "being with" them in their celebrations and struggles, we have a Father who cares about our joys and sorrows. In order to become leaders who follow the example of Jesus, we must first be men and women who share God's heart.

Practical Application for Knowing Your Team

Now that we have discussed what it means for a leader to know his or her team, imagine how it would feel to have a leader who truly sought to know you. Envision a leader who serves you, gives priority to "being with" you, and strives to provide an environment of genuine fellowship when your team gathers together. Think about how refreshing it would be if your leader invited you to dinner and never discussed ministry challenges or opportunities, but instead showed interest in the things of your heart and issues of your spirit. Consider the connection you might experience with a leader who kept up with your interests, your spouse, children, and friends. Imagine how blessed you might feel if your leader remembered your birthday, anniversary, or another significant event in your life. Your heart would undoubtedly be filled with wonder and gratitude for such a leader. You would feel a sense of trust and a certain measure of love for a leader who demonstrated that kind of concern for you and those dearest to you. This is the type of leader that each of us must become as we seek to build a caring, connected team.

As you come to know your team, you will discover that each member has certain relational needs. Each member needs for you to be a part of their world. They need you to give priority to their important relationships, be a part of their celebrations and struggles, and "be with" them as they pursue personal interests and activities. Each team member will need individual attention. They will need for you to convey your interest, concern, and care.

Later in this chapter, we will discuss ten specific relational needs. At this time, you will have the opportunity to practice meeting the relational need of *attention*. As you complete the following exercise, convey appropriate interest and concern as your fellow participants share their responses. Make eye contact, listen carefully to each person's responses, and seek to enter into their world.

After each person shares their current joy or celebration, respond in return. Romans 12:15 tells us to "Rejoice with those who rejoice," so you will want to celebrate with your fellow members. Your rejoicing might sound like, "I'm so happy for you! That's terrific." "I'm thrilled for you. What a blessing from the Lord!"

My Team Journal #1

Let us take a few moments and practice the servanthood we have discussed previously. We want to serve others by getting to know them and expressing love for them. We want to know people in the same way that Jesus did. Take time now to begin to know your team or partner in these ways. Share this information and your reflections with your partner or team. Record the responses of your team below. This will help you remember the significant relationships in their world and what things are most important to them.

Name   Spouse (or close friend if unmarried)   Names & ages of children

_____   _____   _____

_____

My outside interests include _____
One of my current personal struggles or challenges is _____
One of my current joys or celebrations is _____

Name   Spouse (or close friend if unmarried)   Names & ages of children

_____   _____   _____

_____

My outside interests include _____
One of my current personal struggles or challenges is _____
One of my current joys or celebrations is _____

Name   Spouse (or close friend if unmarried)   Names & ages of children

_____   _____   _____

_____

My outside interests include _____
One of my current personal struggles or challenges is _____
One of my current joys or celebrations is _____

Name   Spouse (or close friend if unmarried)   Names & ages of children

_____   _____   _____

_____

My outside interests include _____
One of my current personal struggles or challenges is _____
One of my current joys or celebrations is _____

Name   Spouse (or close friend if unmarried)   Names & ages of children

_____   _____   _____

_____

My outside interests include _____
One of my current personal struggles or challenges is _____
One of my current joys or celebrations is _____

Knowing Their Relational Needs

Relational leaders not only know the interests, struggles, and joys of their team, they deeply know the needs of others. Philippians 4:19 says, "And my God will meet all your needs according to his glorious riches in Christ Jesus." Obviously, the apostle Paul was convinced that we have a "needs-meeting" God—One who possesses both boundless compassion and unlimited resources with which to meet all of our needs.

As human beings, we have physical, spiritual, and relational needs. Everyone is acutely aware that we have an ongoing need for physical nourishment. God, in His sovereignty, elected to meet that need through food and water. In addition, we have a persistent need for rest to renew our strength. God chose to meet this need for physical restoration through the process of nightly sleep. We also share certain spiritual needs. Every person has a need for redemption and the forgiveness of sin. We all have a need for the unconditional love of God because there lays within each of us a deep longing for fellowship with our Creator. Finally, we were all created with certain relational needs. Each of us has an ongoing need for attention, affection, and security in our relationships. Through spiritual maturity, we learn to humbly admit these needs and exercise faith in God's provision. In reality, that is how we experience God's love. We need acceptance, and He gives it (Romans 15:7); we need forgiveness, and He grants it (1 John 1:9); and we need comfort, and He provides it (2 Corinthians 1:3, 4).

But Scripture tells us in Genesis 2 that we not only need a relationship with God, but we require relationships with other people so we will not be alone (Genesis 2:18). But what is it exactly that we need from one another? The Bible again gives us the answer. Romans 15:7 exhorts us to "Accept one another"; Romans 12:10 urges us to "Honor one another"; and 1 Thessalonians 5:11 tells us to "Encourage one another." If Scripture tells us to give these things to each other, it stands to reason that we must need them. We must need acceptance, honor, and encouragement. Take a look at the list of ten key relational needs on the following page. These ten needs have been drawn from the "one another" passages of the Bible. We will give brief attention to all ten needs now, and then delve deeper into a few of the needs in this chapter and those that follow.

TEN KEY RELATIONAL NEEDS

ACCEPTANCE: Receiving one another willingly and unconditionally, especially when one's behavior has been less than perfect (Romans 15:7).

AFFECTION: Expressing care and closeness through appropriate physical touch; saying "I love you" or "I care about you" (Romans 16:16).

APPRECIATION: Expressing thanks, praise, or commendation to one another (Colossians 3:15; 1 Corinthians 11:2).

APPROVAL: Building up and affirming one another; affirming both the fact of and importance of a relationship (Ephesians 4:29).

ATTENTION: Conveying appropriate interest, concern, and care; taking thought of one another; entering another's world (1 Corinthians 12:25).

COMFORT: Responding to a hurting person with words, feelings, and touch; hurting with and for others in the midst of grief or pain (Romans 12:15; 2 Corinthians 1:3, 4).

ENCOURAGEMENT: Urging another to persist and persevere toward a goal; stimulating toward love and good deeds (1 Thessalonians 5:11).

RESPECT: Valuing and regarding one another highly; treating one another as important; honoring one another (Romans 12:10).

SECURITY: Ensuring harmony in relationships; providing freedom from fear or threat of harm (Romans 12:16–18).

SUPPORT: Coming alongside and gently helping with a problem or struggle; providing appropriate assistance (Galatians 6:2).

My Team Journal #2

Refer to the list of ten relational needs again. This time, however, look carefully to see if there is a connection between this list of needs and your responses to Personal Exercise #1. First, look back to see how you completed the sentence: "I sense I am an important part of a team when. . . ." Then try to identify one of the ten needs that corresponds to your answer.

For example, you may have answered, "I sense I am an important part of the team when others ask for my input and seem to value my opinion." This response might correspond with a need for respect. You may sense your importance to the team when others value or regard you highly and thereby meet your need for respect.

Or you may have answered, "I sense I am an important part of the team when we work together to accomplish a task; when everyone shares in the responsibility and success." This response may indicate a need for support. You may sense that you are an important part of a team when others help carry the burden or provide appropriate assistance and meet your need for support.

Share your responses to the following sentences with your group or partner:

I sense that I am important part of the team when. . . . Therefore, it may be important for me to receive _____ (attention, respect, support, etc.).

Take time to record the responses of each group member. This will help you know and remember the specific needs of each person in your team.

Name: _____ Responses: _____

Name: _____ Responses: _____

Name: _____ Responses: _____

Name: _____ Responses: _____

Name: _____ Responses: _____

As you have completed the personal exercises and shared with group members, you have demonstrated the servant's heart of a relational leader. You have entered into another person's world, celebrated with them, and come to know their relational needs, thus learning what it means to "be with" another person. You have begun the process of building a caring and connected team. You have begun to experience the first principle of genuine fellowship. We will now turn our attention to the second principle.

BUILDING A CARING AND CONNECTED TEAM BY LETTING OTHERS KNOW YOU

We learn from the "Good Shepherd" of John 10 that "I know my sheep and **my sheep know me**" (v. 14). Therefore, relational leaders must not only know their team, but must also let their team know them. Once again, Jesus' leadership provides our model.

Being Vulnerable With Your Compassion

One way in which Jesus allowed His team to know Him was by being **vulnerable with His compassion**. He revealed to the disciples His loving concern for the masses: "When he saw the crowds, he had compassion on them, because they were harassed and helpless, like sheep without a shepherd" (Matthew 9:36). Jesus was also transparent in His sorrow for an unbelieving Jerusalem: "O Jerusalem, Jerusalem, you who kill the prophets and stone those sent to you, how often I have longed to gather your children together, as a hen gathers her chicks under her wings, but you were not willing" (23:37). Christ's vulnerable sharing allowed the disciples and the others that followed Him to witness His caring heart and intense love. In order to experience genuine fellowship within a team, the relational leader must do the same. Have you allowed your team to see the tender places of your heart? **Have you been vulnerable with your feelings of compassion?**

Being Vulnerable With Your Dependency

Jesus also allowed the disciples to know Him by being **vulnerable with His dependency.** Christ depended upon the Father at the time of His incarnation: "The Word became flesh and made his dwelling among us. We have seen his glory, the glory of the One and Only, who came from the Father, full of grace and truth" (John 1:14). With dependent love, the Son trusted the Father's heart and plan for the salvation of us all. Later, Jesus revealed His dependence upon the Father in a discourse to His disciples. "I no longer call you servants, because a servant does not know his master's business. Instead, I have called you friends, for everything that I learned from my Father I have made known to you" (15:15). The Son was vulnerable with His team about His reliance on the Father as His daily source of direction and strength. Finally, Jesus showed His team that He depended on the Father for all that He did on earth: "I tell you the truth, the Son can do nothing by himself; he can do only what he sees his Father doing, because whatever the Father does the Son also does" (5:19). The relational leader must also be vulnerable with his or her trust in the Lord. Have you revealed your own inadequacies to your team and shared how you are counting on God? **Have you been vulnerable with your own dependency upon the Father?**

Being Vulnerable With Your Need for Support

Jesus also allowed His team to know Him by being **vulnerable with His need for support**. He did not hesitate to call upon the disciples for assistance in ministering to the needs of others. For example, He asked the disciples to handle the distribution of the loaves and fish at the feeding of the five thousand: "Then he gave them to the disciples, and the disciples gave them to the people" (Matthew 14:19). Jesus also vulnerably shared His personal need for prayer and support during His most agonizing hours: "My soul is overwhelmed with sorrow to the point of death. Stay here and keep watch with me" (26:38). This garden scene is not an account of One who wanted to model an effective prayer life. Rather, it depicts a Savior who was vulnerably expressing His need for the disciples to "be with" Him and share His pain. The relational leader must also be vulnerable with his or her need for support. Have you let others know that you rely on their help? **Have you shared your own struggles and communicated ways in which others could help you carry these burdens?**

Being Vulnerable With Your Pain

Finally, Jesus allowed the disciples to know Him by being **vulnerable with His pain.** With a sorrowful heart, Christ expressed to Philip the pain He felt over not being fully known by His disciples: "Don't you know me, Philip, even after I have been among you such a long time? Anyone who has seen me has seen the Father. How can you say, 'Show us the Father?'" (John 14:9). Jesus was grieved as it became apparent that the disciples had missed much of what He had tried to communicate. Christ's heart was heavy because they had missed knowing Him. In the Garden, Christ shared His hurt with Peter, James, and John when they failed to give Him support and demonstrate care: "'Could you men not keep watch with me for one hour?'" (Matthew 26:40). The Savior asked His closest friends to share His burden as He faced the inevitability of the Cross, and the three had fallen asleep. Jesus vulnerably shared His pain and disappointment with His followers. Relational leaders must also learn to be vulnerable with personal pain. Have you been free to tell others how your heart has been hurt? **Are you able to share your emotional pain with your team?**

Just as Christ made it a priority to let the disciples know Him, so He also vulnerably reveals Himself to us. Vulnerability relates to the Hebrew word *sod*, which means "to reveal; disclose." God has allowed us to know Him by revealing and disclosing His thoughts, feelings, and character through His Word and the life of His Son. The wise sage noted, "[God] is intimate with the upright" (Proverbs 3:32 NASB). God allows those who have a personal relationship with Him to share in the very depths of His love.

God's Word also reveals His commitment to vulnerability in its portrayals of biblical leaders. Have you ever wondered why we have been presented with such stark, uncompromising views of all the heroes in the Bible? We see not only their strengths, but their weaknesses and shortcomings as well. We see the strength of Moses as he leads the children of Israel out of Egypt, contrasted with his impulsive nature when He strikes the rock (Exodus 14:21; Numbers 20:11). We witness Elijah's boldness as he confronts the prophets of Baal, yet we get a glimpse of his fear as he runs from Queen Jezebel (1 Kings 18 and 19). We must ask ourselves, "Why did God allow us to see their failures? Why did the Lord let us examine their faults and witness their weakness?" In part, it is because God wants to give us a glimpse of the power of vulnerability. He wants us to see that when we are weak, His Spirit brings forth strength: "My power is made perfect in weakness" (2 Corinthians 12:9).

Now that we have explored various ways in which a leader should demonstrate vulnerability, imagine how you would be impacted by a leader who allowed you to fully know him. Imagine a leader who is vulnerable with feelings of compassion, one who shares with you those things that burden his or her heart. Think about how blessed you would feel as you came to know your leader as one whose heart is tender and caring. Consider what it would be like to have a leader who shares his or her need for support, one who trusts you with issues of the heart and spirit. Think about how approachable this kind of leader would seem as you came to know him or her as someone with real needs and real struggles. Consider how much more fully you could trust a leader who allowed you to know his or her personal pain. Such vulnerability would prompt a certain level of security and feeling of connection as you came to know your leader's true heart.

Practical Application for Letting Your Team Know You

During the next exercise, you will have the opportunity to know your team and let them know you. It will be important to meet one another's need for acceptance as you verbalize your responses. Your group members will need to sense that others will receive them unconditionally, even if their behavior is less than perfect. You will have the opportunity to "accept one another . . . as Christ accepted you" (Romans 15:7). Christ accepted you while you were still a sinner (5:8), without judgment, criticism, or condemnation. Now you will have the opportunity to give to others what you have received from the Lord.

You will need an environment that is a safe place for vulnerable sharing. To create such an environment, you will first want to give appropriate eye contact, listen attentively without interruption, and then respond with accepting words. As you hear your partner or other group members' responses, be on guard for any thoughts you may have that are judgmental or critical. Be especially careful to refrain from such thoughts as you hear about struggles that are very different from your own. By contrast, you will want to express thoughts and words that are accepting and caring, like, "I'm so glad you shared that with us. Thank you for your vulnerability," or "I can sense how difficult this situation has been for you. I would have responded in the same way."

My Team Journal #3

As relational leaders who desire to serve others as Christ did, we will want to love others by letting them know us. We will want to be like the "Good Shepherd" who lets the sheep know Him.

Let us take the opportunity to be known and demonstrate care as we complete the following sentences:

I have felt compassion recently for . . .
(For example: *my teenage daughter as she struggles to be accepted by her peer group*).

I have been depending on God for . . .
(For example: *the courage to address a growth area with a friend*).

I have needed support recently in . . .
(For example: *managing some financial debt*).

I have recently experienced emotional pain about . . .
(For example: *being misunderstood by my neighbor*).

Prepare your own answers to these sentences and share them with your partner or team.

Be sure to give accepting responses as each person finishes their time of sharing.

Make brief notes about the responses of other members. This will allow you to know each person in a more meaningful way and help you remember their important feelings and emotions. You will also refer to these responses in a later exercise.

Name: _____ Responses: _____

Name: _____ Responses: _____

Name: _____ Responses: _____

Name: _____ Responses: _____

Name: _____ Responses: _____

As you deepen the vulnerability within your team, you also deepen trust. You undoubtedly felt more connected as you humbled yourselves and shared together. Each of you has now experienced an additional dimension of fellowship as you were vulnerable with one another and met the need for acceptance. The Lord is blessed by your humility and is glorified by your accepting responses. "Accept one another as Christ has accepted you, **to the glory of God**" (see Romans 15:7). You are blessed because you have deepened your love for others and furthered your experience of true fellowship. Now let us look at the final principle for building a caring and connected team.

BUILDING A CARING AND CONNECTED TEAM BY SACRIFICIALLY LOVING ONE ANOTHER

John 10:14, 15 tells us that Jesus not only knows His sheep and lets His sheep know Him, He **lays down His life for the sheep**. Jesus, our attentive shepherd, gives to us sacrificially and loves us extravagantly. The psalmist speaks of Christ's involvement in our lives and illustrates His sacrificial care in a variety of ways: "He makes me to lie down in green pastures, he leads me beside quiet waters, he restores my soul. He guides me . . . He is with me . . . His rod and staff comfort me . . . He prepares a table before me . . . He anoints my head with oil" (see Psalm 23). This psalm reassures us that the Good Shepherd is fully engaged and deeply involved in our lives. Jesus allows us to enjoy the good things of life, brings us contentment and rest, and provides refreshment and well-being, all because He cares. The Good Shepherd gives guidance, protection, security from harm, and intimate relationship because of His great love for His "sheep."

Jesus' Sacrificial Love for the Disciples

During those first two years of His ministry, Jesus was deeply involved in the lives of His disciples. This involvement was always for their benefit and always motivated by care. We've already witnessed Christ's care for Peter in the healing of his mother-in-law (Mark 1:29–31). Jesus also demonstrated His compassion for the disciples in the calming of the storm. "Jesus was in the stern, sleeping on a cushion. The disciples woke him and said to him, 'Teacher, don't you care if we drown?'" (4:38). Jesus got up, rebuked the wind, and said to the waves, "Be still!" (v. 39). Even though the disciples seemed to doubt the Lord's concern, His care for them was ever-present and continuously abundant. The disciples apparently forgot that Christ had promised to take them to the other side of the lake (v. 35).

Our Calling and Motivation to Sacrificially Love Our Team

The relational leader must also become caringly involved in the lives of his or her team. We must give sacrificially to team members and set aside time for these relationships. This involvement must be motivated not by a sense of duty or obligation, but by Christlike compassion and care. **Have you prioritized relationships with your team members just because you love them?**

Just as Christ was caringly involved with the disciples, we have a God who is caringly involved with us. The Hebrew word for "caring involvement" is *sakan*. The Psalmist wrote of God's loving engagement in our lives: "[You] are intimately acquainted with all my ways" (Psalm 139:3 NASB). Notice the breadth of this acquaintance: with **all** my ways. He knows all our failures, faults, and shortcomings, yet He still cares! This Hebrew word also answers the question, "Why does God want to know us?" What is His motive? Is it to judge us? Criticize us? Condemn us? Far from it! He wants to be intimately acquainted with us, to know us deeply, so that He can express the tender care that is at the very heart of His nature. Relational leaders must also exhibit this loving engagement. **Have you communicated with words or actions, "I want to know my team so that I can better care for them"? Have your team members sensed that your involvement in their lives is motivated by a love from the Lord?**

Now that we have defined caring involvement, can you imagine how blessed you would feel to have a leader who wants to know you so that she can better care for you? Imagine a leader who loves you despite the fact that she knows your failures, faults, and shortcomings. That kind of leader would create an environment of genuine care and emotional safety. You could feel safe following her because you would be confident of her motives and assured of her efforts on your behalf.

Practical Application of Caring Involvement

One of the most valuable opportunities you will have to become caringly involved with your team will be during times of emotional pain or hurt. In the following exercise, you will have the chance to practice your caring involvement as you meet the need of comfort for one another. The Greek word for comfort is *parakaleo*, which means "to come to one's side, to one's aid," and suggests the ability to console and give help. As you reflect on the responses you heard in My Team Journal #3, you will now be able to console or come alongside one another and give aid.

Take time to meet the need for comfort of each partner or member of your group. Look back to the notes you made as you heard each person give their responses to My Team Journal #3. What did you feel for each person as you heard them share? What did it do to your heart to hear their need for support, area of dependence, emotional pain, or feelings of deep compassion for others? As you identify your feelings for this other person, you are ready to share directly with them. Your comforting words might be something like, "I'm so sorry that happened. It hurts me to hear the pain in your voice," or "My heart hurts when I think about you feeling discouraged and alone."

In His Word, God tells us that He cares for us and provides loving comfort so that we, in turn, can comfort others (2 Corinthians 1:3, 4). This is your opportunity to offer the same solace that God has given to you and become caringly involved with one another. Pause now and allow Christ to bring to your heart a sense of empathy and compassion for your partner or group members. Ask Him to remind you of the specific things each person said and the feelings they conveyed. Now, ask Christ to remind you of what He was feeling as each person shared. What did Jesus feel for your partner or group members? What might He then prompt **you** to feel for them?

Experiencing the Word Together #2

"Mourn with those who mourn" (Romans 12:15).

Reflect on the shared responses to My Team Journal #3. Pray for the Spirit's prompting to care as you complete the sentence below:

I hurt with _____ *concerning* _____.

(For example: *I hurt with John concerning the difficulties with his daughter.*)
(For example: *I hurt with Kathy concerning her financial stress.*)

Now take turns sharing these responses with one another. Speak directly to one another. Share how it makes you feel to hear of each person's pain, struggle, life stress, or need for support. Express what it does to your heart to learn of their hurt.

I want you to know that I felt _____ *as I heard you share about . . .*

I hurt with you as I heard you say . . .

(For example: *John, I want you to know that I felt great compassion as I heard you share about your daughter. I saw how much it was grieving you to be estranged from her. I hurt with you as I heard you say how much you miss her.*)

(For example: *Kathy, I want you to know that I felt sad as I heard you share about your financial stress. I heard the strain in your voice and could imagine how scary it must be for you. I hurt with you when I heard you say that all of this has made it difficult to trust.*)

As you have worked through the exercises and in this chapter, you have expressed the humility of a servant, "been with" other people, and demonstrated care for one another. You experienced the first part of Romans 12:15 as you rejoiced with one another. You experienced

Romans 15:7 as you accepted one another. Romans 12:15 and 2 Corinthians 1:2–4 were lived out as you comforted others with the same comfort you have received from God. Loving care was demonstrated as you encountered 1 Corinthians 12:25 and met one another's need for attention. You have come to know others, let them know you, and become caringly involved in their lives. This is what the early church called *koinonia,* or fellowship. The fellowship you have been a part of today is much deeper than shared refreshments or after-church social events. This fellowship brings glory and pleasure to God as you live out His Word together.

We have successfully embodied these biblical principles here with one another, but what will preserve this spirit of care as we lead and serve on a daily basis? Once again, sheer determination won't sustain us. Adequate insight and knowledge won't keep us loving one another. We can only depend on the love of the Father. You have received the heavenly Father's divine caring involvement today. Imagine that: your heavenly Father has demonstrated His love for you today—through the gentle responses of those around you. It was actually Jesus who was knowing you and caring for you through your partners and group members.

Now, as you have received abundantly from the heavenly Father, He will produce in you a grateful heart that overflows in selfless giving. It is this moment-by-moment thankfulness that will prompt you to serve. It is this unbounded grace that will empower your intimate care for others. It is this amazing gift that will fuel your longing to truly know this One who loves you so completely.

Chapter 4 Outline

Personal Exercise #1

I. Reaffirming the Priority of "Being With" Before "Sending Out"

  A. The Disciples' Possible Reactions

    1. Peter—impulsive, impatient, pridefully over-confident

    2. Philip—rational, organizing, concern for the practical "how-to's"

    3. James and John—competitive, wanting recognition

Personal Exercise #2

  B. Jesus' Care for the Disciples' Concerns (Mark 1:29–31)

  C. Jesus' Care for Our Concerns: "Cast all your anxiety upon Him because he cares for you" (1 Peter 5:7).

Experiencing the Word Together #1

II. Building a Caring and Connected Team by Knowing Them

  A. Knowing About Their Important Relationships

    1. Names of spouse (if married), close friends, etc.

    2. Names, ages, interests of children

    3. Any other relationships important to each of your team members

    4. Initiate "being with" team members and "important others."

  B. Knowing About Their Interests and Activities

    1. How do team members spend leisure time?

    2. What are their hobbies?

3. What recreation do they most enjoy?

4. Initiate "being with" team members in their activities or interests.

C. Knowing About Their Celebrations and Struggles

1. Are we aware when they or those they love have positive experiences?

2. Do we know when team members or those they love are struggling?

My Team Journal #1—Getting to Know Each Other

D. Knowing Their Relational Needs

1. We all have needs—physical, spiritual, and relational, and God is committed to meeting them:

"And my God will meet all your needs according to His glorious riches in Christ Jesus" (Philippians 4:19). This verse makes no sense if we don't have any needs!

2. What are our most significant relational needs?

My Team Journal #2—Identifying Priority Needs

III. Building a Caring and Connected Team by Letting Them Know You

A. Being Vulnerable with Your Compassion

B. Being Vulnerable with Your Dependency

C. Being Vulnerable with Your Need for Support

D. Being Vulnerable with Your Pain

My Team Journal #3—Helping Others Know You

IV. Building a Caring and Connected Team by Sacrificially Loving One Another

A. Jesus' Sacrificial Love for the Disciples

1. Healing Peter's mother-in-law (Mark 1:29–31)

    2. Calming the storm (Mark 4:35–41)

    3. What were some other times Jesus cared for His followers?

B. Our Calling and Motivation to Sacrificially Love Our Team

    1. Have we prioritized relationships with team members just because we love them?

    2. Have we communicated with words and actions, "I want to know my team so that I can better care for them"?

Experiencing The Word Together #2

Additional Resources

George Barna, *The Power of Team Leadership: Achieving Success Through Shared Responsibility* (Colorado Springs: Waterbrook Press, 2001).

Dietrich Bonhoeffer, *Life Together* (New York: Harper and Row, 1954).

Daniel Coleman, *Emotional Intelligence* (New York: Bantam Books, 1995).

Daniel Coleman, *Working with Emotional Intelligence* (New York: Bantam Books, 1998).

David Ferguson, *The Great Commandment Principle* (Wheaton, IL: Tyndale House Publishers, Inc., 1998).

David and Teresa Ferguson, *Never Alone* (Wheaton, IL: Tyndale House Publishers, Inc., 2001).

Kenneth O. Gangel, *Team Leadership in Christian Ministry: Using Multiple Gifts to Build a Unified Vision* (Chicago: Moody Press, 1997).

John C. Maxwell, *The Twenty One Indispensable Qualities of a Leader* (Nashville: Thomas Nelson, 1999).

Chapter 5

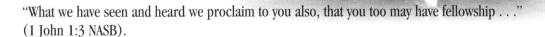

Gaining Freedom to Become Relational Leaders

"What we have seen and heard we proclaim to you also, that you too may have fellowship . . ." (1 John 1:3 NASB).

As the Apostle John reflected on the purpose of his proclamations and writings, he boldly asserted that the ultimate aim of them was that we might have fellowship. In the previous chapter, we experienced a taste of true *koinonia* through knowing and caring for one another. In this chapter, we will have the opportunity to "become mature, attaining to the whole measure of the fullness of Christ" (Ephesians 4:13) as we examine three critical goals of fellowship that give insight into why the apostle placed such a clear emphasis on our relationships with one another and with God. We will see how our times of fellowship can enable us to see God more clearly, become secure in our identity, and grow more committed to our life purpose of loving others. Each of these three goals, in turn, brings freedom from the hindrances that often distract us from serving others.

WE GAIN FREEDOM TO BECOME RELATIONAL LEADERS BY HAVING AN ACCURATE VIEW OF GOD.

In one of the defining moments of his ministry, Jesus was asked by one of the religious leaders of His day which commandment was the greatest. Christ gave an unexpected reply: "'Hear, O Israel, the Lord our God, the Lord is one. Love the Lord your God with all your heart and with all your soul and with all your mind and with all your strength.' The second is this: 'Love your neighbor as yourself.' There is no commandment greater than these" (Mark 12:29–31).

This Great Commandment to love God and love people defines the true identity of those who are called His church and those who are called to be leaders. Great Commandment love must be at the heart of who we are and what we do. Yet every individual who seeks to live out this commandment will discover a significant challenge: We must love the **real** God with all our heart, soul, mind, and strength. In other words, we will never be able to experience Great Commandment love for God unless we have a clear view of who He really is. If we were to examine ourselves, many of us would discover that our view of God often impedes our ability to love Him and other people.

> **Our view of God often impedes our ability to love Him and other people.**

How Do You View God?

It is important for each of us to closely examine his or her own concept of God. How do you really see Him? The following Personal Exercise will help you address this question.

Personal Exercise #1

Imagine this scene: It has been a particularly hard day. You had a terrible argument with a family member in the morning and said some things in anger that you really regret. Later in the day, you discovered that not only did you not get the promotion at work you had anticipated, but also that the company is contemplating a lay-off. Next, the school principal called and asked for an appointment so the two of you could discuss disciplinary action for your child. Finally, you left for the weekly church meeting only to find a flat tire on your car with no spare in the trunk. After having suffered through such a horrific day, you "lost it" with the guy from the auto shop when he tried to overcharge you for the repair.

Now, imagine walking into your church and meeting Jesus in the hallway. He is actually standing next to you. Freeze that moment in time. What is your heart saying now? How does it feel to see Jesus on a day like this? Are you afraid He will lecture you about all the things you did wrong that day and how you could have done it better? Are you concerned that He will shake His head in disappointment and utter the words, "How many times have I told you . . ."? Are you worried that He will walk past you and not even notice the stress on your face or the sadness in your eyes? Or are you perhaps scared that He might notice those things but not take time to care?

Your answers to the questions above give an indication of your concept of God. The voice you hear in your heart and the words you imagine Christ speaking to you reflect your view of Him. God cares deeply about your image of Him and longs for you to see Him as He really is. Could it be that God, the **real** God, might have this to say after a difficult day? *My precious child, I am so saddened by the difficulties you experienced. Please tell me about the events of your day because I care for you. I was there right beside you each time you felt frustration, disappointment, sadness, or defeat, and my heart hurt for you. I don't want to give you a lecture or sermon. I did notice some of the responses that you must wish you could take back, but I am not disappointed or disgusted with you as a person. You are my child. I noticed the deep pain you felt, and I was moved with compassion. I want to wrap my arms around you and reassure you of my love.*

If your view of God is inconsistent with the one above, then you may not be seeing the real God. If your God would have something significantly different to say, you may not have a true picture of God's heart for you and His deep longing to care. You would probably find it very difficult to love a god who did not respond to you with love and compassion.

Most of us have a somewhat "mixed up" view of God. Sometimes we see Him as He really is, and at other times our vision is impaired. It is important to explore some of these hindrances that we encounter.

Pause now and reflect on your view of God. In our imaginary scene, what words did you expect Christ to say as He met you in that hallway? What was the expression on the face of Jesus as He talked with you? How did He respond to you?

Complete the sentences that follow:

I might, at times, expect Jesus to say . . .

I might, at times, expect Christ to respond with . . .

I may sometimes be hindered in experiencing God as He really is because I see Him as . . .

Share your view of God with at least one other participant or with your small group (as directed by your leader).

My Team Journal #1

Record your team members' responses to Personal Exercise #1.

Name: _____ Responses: _____

Name: _____ Responses: _____

Name: _____ Responses: _____

Name: _____ Responses: _____

Name: _____ Responses: _____

Hopefully, each of you discovered some of the inaccuracies in your concept of God and recognized how they might impede your ability to love Him. Now imagine how these things might also affect your ability to **lead**. The following section will illustrate how our view of God impacts our decision-making ability and often determines how we treat the people we lead.

Our View of God Can Impact Our Leadership.

The Example of King Saul. We see the impact of an inaccurate concept of God as we look at King Saul's leadership. First Samuel 13:1–15 details some of the leadership decisions of King Saul and reveals that the king must have seen God as distant and uninvolved in the lives of His people. As Saul prepared to lead the people of Israel into battle with the Philistines, Scripture tells us that all the troops were quaking with fear because they were so outnumbered by the enemy. Because of his own fear, Saul doubted God's willingness or ability to act on Israel's behalf and went against the prophet Samuel's instructions. Saul offered sacrifices himself in an attempt to gain the Lord's favor. As a result of his actions, Samuel let the king know that his kingdom would no longer endure and that there would be no dynasty bearing his name. We see further evidence of Saul's inability to see and experience the real God when he gave David increasing responsibility in the kingdom yet became jealous of David's success (18:5–9). We also know that Saul was so hindered in his concept of God that he attempted to take David's life and ultimately ended his own (19:11, 31:4). Saul's view of God made it difficult for him to see a God who would protect and provide for His people. Saul was not able to trust God to intervene on his behalf. He was not free to make wise, faith-filled choices or to demonstrate the loving heart of a relational leader.

The Example of King David. In contrast to King Saul, David illustrated leadership that was positively impacted by an accurate view of God. David's decision-making reflected an accurate view of God even as a young boy, when he chose to fight Goliath (1 Samuel 17:1–59). We observe David's confidence in God when he responded to Saul's doubts about his ability to defeat the Philistine by proclaiming, "The Lord who delivered me from the paw of the lion and the paw of the bear will deliver me from the hand of this Philistine" (v. 37). Later, as we witness David's attempts to relate to King Saul, we see how his view of God impacted his ability to love. David had the opportunity to harm Saul, but he chose to let God bring vengeance. Because David saw God as a God of protection, he trusted Him to avenge the deeds of Saul, saying, "May the Lord judge between you and me. And may the Lord avenge the wrongs you have done to me, but my hand will not touch you" (24:12). Consequently, even Saul recognized David's relationship with the Lord and acknowledged the certainty of David's success: "May the Lord reward you well for the way you treated me today. I know that you will surely be king and that the kingdom of Israel will be established in your hands" (v. 19, 20).

The lives of these two Old Testament kings illustrate how our view of God can affect our ability to lead. Relational leaders must see God for who He really is if they are to become equipped to handle the inevitable challenges of leadership, and if they are to experience the freedom to lead and love others as Christ did.

Hindered Views of God

Now that we have examined the stark contrast between leaders with an accurate view of God and those with flawed views of Him, we must examine some common views of God that obscure His true character. The following Personal Exercise will help us examine some of these hindered views of God, and evaluate the impact they might be having on our lives and ministries.

Personal Exercise #2

Take a moment now and reflect on your view of God again. How do you see Him?

For a moment, put yourself in one of the Bible stories we often tell our children. It is the story of Zacchaeus. The Gospel of Luke tells us that there was a wealthy tax collector named Zacchaeus who lived in the city of Jericho. Zacchaeus wanted to see Jesus as He passed through the town one day; but being a short man, he could not see over the crowd. So the tax collector climbed a sycamore tree in order to get a better view. When Jesus reached Zacchaeus, He immediately asked to go to the tax collector's house. This invitation was especially significant because of the reputation of tax collectors in Christ's day. They were considered traitors to the people of Israel because they collected taxes for the Roman government. Furthermore, Zacchaeus was a wealthy man; and because of the corrupt system of his day, he most certainly obtained this wealth by cheating, stealing, and embezzling money. Yet Christ chose to spend time with this man who was hated and despised by most of the Jews (Luke 19:1–10).

In many ways we are like Zacchaeus. We have done things we regret, hurt others by our choices, and lived lives that are far from perfect. We at times, have failed, sinned and made poor choices. Perhaps we have "blown it" again and again. Now imagine yourself sitting in the top of a tree, waiting for Jesus. He walks toward you, stops just below the tree, and looks up. How would He respond? Would He look up at you and shake His finger with words of condemnation? Would He look up at you and shake His head in disappointment? Or would He just pass you by, barely noticing you or your needs?

Take a moment to identify your response to the questions above. Then consider three of the most common hindered views of God and how they might impact our ability to love Him.

Some of us might see an **Inspecting God.** He seems to have a "heavenly tally sheet" and is just waiting to record what we do. An inspecting god examines our every motive and behavior. He then relates to us according to how many good or bad marks we have accumulated.

This type of god waits to catch us doing something we shouldn't. It is difficult to love a god like that. Imagine trying to love someone who only examined you and often pointed out what you did wrong.

Others may view God as a **Disappointed God.** This type of god notices our behavior and shakes his head in disappointment or even disgust. He keeps his arms crossed as he looks down at our feeble attempts to live a righteous life. This kind of god might shrug his shoulders and walk out of the room because, ultimately, he has given up on us. No matter how many positive things we try to do or how good we try to become, this kind of god tells us that it is never enough. We are **never** good enough. Imagine trying to love someone like that—someone who you could never please. It would be extremely difficult to maintain a loving relationship with a god like that.

At other times, we might view God as a **Distant God,** or even a god who is completely uninvolved in our lives. This type of god is too busy to notice our concerns and seems to take little interest in us. He does not appear to have time for people like us because he only takes care of the important things. This kind of god listens with one ear as we pray, giving only half-hearted attention. He seems detached and perhaps a little too distracted to care. Imagine trying to love a god like that. Imagine trying to love someone who barely noticed you or was always too busy to talk with you. That kind of relationship would be difficult to sustain.

As we consider these flawed views of God, it is important for us to realize that, as leaders, we are at risk of treating others in the same way that we perceive God treating us. If a leader views God as an inspecting God, he or she might tend to inspect others. If a leader sees God as a disappointed God who is difficult to please, he or she may find it hard to communicate that others are ever "good enough." Likewise, if leaders see God as distant and uninvolved, they may tend to distance themselves from those they lead and may become fearful or controlling.

We must again emphasize that the relational leader gives priority to knowing the **real** God. The real God wants a relationship with us. He is attentive and caring. He does not sit in heaven with a tally sheet or get preoccupied with more important things. He wants to be close. He wants to be your intimate friend (Proverbs 3:32). He is excited when you wake up in the morning because He cannot wait to talk with you and relate to you. He is delighted to know you and be with you (Psalm 147:11). He generously and graciously gave up His Son because

He could not bear the thought of eternity without you (Romans 8:32). The real God is able to separate who you **are** as His beloved child, from what you might **do**. He is pleased with you because He sees you with the eyes of a Master Creator—One who admires His handiwork and values each of His treasures because they are unique and wonderful (Psalm 139:13, 14).

We see confirmation of the real God's character in the story of Zacchaeus. Scripture tells us that Zacchaeus responded to the Savior's invitation by coming down at once and welcoming Jesus gladly. His heart was thrilled to have the opportunity to be with the Lord. Jesus knew what Zacchaeus had **done**, but his loving response focused on who he **was** and who he would become.

Reflect on your own "hindered" concept of God. How do you sometimes see Him?

I may sometimes see God as _____ (*inspecting, distant, detached, disappointed, disapproving,* or other specific descriptors of your choice) *because I often imagine Him . . .*

My view of God as _____ *could impact my decision making by . . .*
(For example: *My view of God as distant could impact my ability to make wise decisions by making me fearful. I've realized that when I am not sure God is interested in and attentive to my needs, I become easily overwhelmed. Those feelings can paralyze my ability to make decisions.*)

My view of God as _____ *could influence the way I relate to others by . . .*
(For example: *My view of God as an inspecting god could influence the way I relate to others by causing me to sometimes be overly critical and harsh.*)

Share your responses with a partner or small group as directed by your facilitator.

My Team Journal #2

Record your team members' responses to Personal Exercise #2.

Name: _____ Responses: _____

Name: _____ Responses: _____

Name: _____ Responses: _____

Name: _____ Responses: _____

Name: _____ Responses: _____

You may be asking yourself, "Since I have realized that I sometimes do not have an accurate view of God, how do I change that? How do I begin to see the real God so that I can love Him and other people?" Critical ingredients for changing our view of God are found within the fellowship of the body of Christ.

Experiencing True Fellowship Allows Us to See the Real God.

"No one has ever seen God; but if we love one another, God lives in us and his love is made complete in us" (1 John 4:12).

One of the critical goals of fellowship is that we would live and love in a way that helps those around us experience Christ as He really is. As we gather together in leadership teams, small groups, and close relationships, we need to challenge and encourage one another to see God for who He really is. We must ask ourselves: Are the people that make up our team, small group, or accountability partnership living and loving in a way that enables us to see God in one another? Are we living and loving so that the world is able to see God for who He really is? Are we loving one another so well that all men will know that we are His disciples (John 13:35)?

How can we encourage and challenge one another so that we gain the freedom and ability to see the real God? We can let others see God when someone fails and we accept them as in Romans 15:7. When someone shares a struggle and we encourage them as in Hebrews 10:25, we demonstrate the heart of the real God. When someone is lonely and we care for them as in I Corinthians 12:25, they will come to know and see God for who He really is. You have the chance to let others see God by communicating reassurance to them, to let the love of God be perfected in you (1 John 4:12), and to become living epistles of Christ's care.

Experiencing the Word Together #1

"Let the beloved of the Lord rest secure in Him" (Deuteronomy 33:12).

As you heard each member of your group share their responses to the exercises above, you undoubtedly learned of some of their most tender places of hurt. As each person talked about their view of God, they were possibly revealing some of their most critical areas of pain. For instance, if one of your partners said they often see a God who is distant or neglectful, this person may have significant areas of emotional pain, possibly due to relationships that were distant or neglectful. If one of your partners said they often see God as critical or condemning, they may have had several human relationships that were filled with criticism and condemnation.

Since your partners or group members may have just shared significant areas of hurt, you should take this opportunity to show your care and concern. Reflect back on the responses of your partner or small group. How do they see God? What sources of pain or hurt did they reveal and how does that make you feel?

Respond with care and comfort to one another. Your comfort might sound like . . .

It hurt my heart to hear you say that you sometimes saw God as _____. I'm guessing that means that you have had other people in your life who treated you in this same manner. That makes me very sad.

It saddens me to know that you sometimes see a God who _____. I regret that for you.

It is important to realize that your partners and team members have just shared how you might best demonstrate love for them. If your partner sees God as critical and condemning, then you can demonstrate how much you love him or her by offering words of acceptance and approval rather than criticism or condemnation. If your partner sees God as distant and neglectful, then you might best love this person by taking interest in them, by being attentive and responsive to their needs.

Take the next few moments and meet the need of **security** for each partner or person in your group. *Security* means "to be free from harm" or "to be certain of harmony in a relationship." Therefore, you will want to reassure each partner or team member that they can rest secure in their relationship with you.

Reflect again on each person's view of God and then respond with words of loving reassurance.

_____, *you can be assured that I want to express Christ's love to you by . . .*
  Participant's Name

(For example: *Mary, you can be assured that I want to express Christ's love to you by becoming more sensitive. I do not want to respond with criticism or condemnation. Instead, I will be careful to always "build you up.")*

(For example: *Bob, you can be assured that I want to express Christ's love to you by being attentive and responsive to your needs. I will ask more often about your life interests, and I really want to hear your answers. I want to know about your true feelings and needs.)*

Share your responses with a partner or group members as directed by your facilitator.

Take note that your experiences above are a part of what it "looks like" to see God through other people and to have His love made complete in us (1 John 4:12).

Now that we have addressed the first struggle that often hinders relational leaders from accomplishing their goals, let us focus on a second struggle that seems to particularly plague our Western culture.

WE GAIN FREEDOM TO BECOME RELATIONAL LEADERS BY EMBRACING OUR IDENTITY AS THE BELOVED OF GOD.

Just as realtional leaders must see God as He really is, so we must also see ourselves as God sees us—as His beloved children.

How Do We Define Our Value and Worth?

We live in a world that operates on the premise of "doing things" in order to be "OK." We work hard to keep jobs and work even harder to get raises. Many leaders struggle with the belief that their worth is determined by what they do and how well they do it. They tend to equate "what I do" with "who I am." Leaders who are not free to see their identity as the beloved of God may have an inconsistent sense of well-being that fluctuates according to their levels of "doing." Leaders who are not free to embrace their identity may also often be critical of themselves or other people and may exhibit a strong drive to perform. Finally, we may find that leaders who have not claimed their identity may be overly sensitive and defensive and may frequently personalize any feedback about their performance that is less than outstanding.

> **Many people are hindered in their leadership because they are uncertain of their identity as the beloved of God.**

Larry and Sharon know what it is like to struggle with issues of performance and self-worth. Their marriage has suffered because of Larry's consistent belief that unless he does things perfectly, there must be something wrong with him. While the couples in Larry and Sharon's class feel blessed by their ministry, Larry privately struggles with taking many of their comments personally. He tries to hide the agony he feels when anyone gives feedback about a lesson that is anything less than "glowing." If something goes wrong in one of his areas of responsibility, Larry immediately concludes, "It must be my fault." If he misunderstands the instructions for implementing new attendance procedures or forgets to make the announcement about the New Membership class, Larry immediately gets defensive. He privately scolds himself for not doing things better or not teaching a lesson perfectly. Larry, like many of us, is hindered in his leadership because he is uncertain about his identity as the beloved of God. He is not free to lead others as effectively as he might wish because of his struggle with his own worth and identity.

God Separates Our Worth From Our Performance.

The Apostle Peter seemed to have something in common with Larry and with many of us. He too was often preoccupied with performance rather than being confident in who he was in Christ. We know from Scripture that Peter was certainly a man of action, one who consistently displayed a headstrong, impetuous nature. On the Mount of Transfiguration, Peter was more concerned about building tabernacles for Christ than rejoicing with Him over the opportunity to be with Moses and Elijah (Matthew 17:4). In the upper room, Peter initially refused to let Jesus wash his feet, stubbornly resisting the Savior's demonstration of love (John 13:6–11). In the garden, Peter defended Jesus by impulsively cutting off a servant's ear (18:10). Finally, after having arrogantly announced that he was willing to die for Jesus, Peter denied even knowing Him (18:17, 25–27). These actions reveal that Peter struggled at various times with both pride and a sense of unworthiness. In either case, his own estimation of himself rarely corresponded with the way that Christ saw him.

Jesus lovingly separated Peter's personal worth from his performance when He gave him his new name: "Blessed are you, Simon son of Jonah, for this was not revealed to you by man, but by my Father in heaven. And I tell you that you are Peter, and on this rock I will build my church" (Matthew 16:17, 18). Even as Christ predicted Peter's denial, He also graciously promised to pray for Peter, restore him, and use him to strengthen others (Luke 22:31, 32).

Can you imagine what it was like for Peter to live with the knowledge that he had denied the Savior? The reports of Jesus' gruesome death must have tormented him as he recalled his rash vow that he would die before he would abandon Christ. He probably heard roosters crowing in his dreams. But imagine how he must have felt when he heard the report of the women who found Jesus' tomb empty. Undoubtedly, they told him that the angel of the Lord had mentioned Peter by name when he instructed the women to spread the news to the disciples (Mark 16:7). Perhaps this was Christ's way of emphasizing to Peter that he was still loved, still accepted, still an important member of the team. Luke tells us that, while some of the other disciples dismissed the women's story, Peter *ran* to the tomb, no doubt hoping against hope that it was true (Luke 24:10–12).

Later, on the beaches of Galilee, Jesus commissioned Peter to tend His flock and build His church (John 21:15–22). Christ did not reward Peter according to what he had done, but according to his identity as the "beloved of God." This declaration of Peter's worth, apart from his performance, helped prepare him to be the leader of the believers in Jerusalem and gave him the courage to assist in shepherding the early church following the Day of Pentecost. The knowledge that Christ loved and trusted him in spite of his behavior must have been a source of great strength to Peter.

Many of us need to receive this same freedom from performance-based worth. We need to experience the impact of Romans 5:8: "But God demonstrates his own love for us in this: While we were still sinners, Christ died for us." The most beautiful part of this verse is the word "while." It does not say that God demonstrates His love for you *after* you "shape up." It does not say God demonstrates His love for you *reluctantly* because He already knows you will likely blow it again and again. It says that God loved us for who He saw we were in Christ, *while* we were still sinners. His love has nothing to do with us, and everything to do with Him.

The Fruit of Being Secure in Our Identity

Even though we see evidence of Peter's struggle with self-worth, we also know that Peter later grew certain of his identity as a beloved son of God. He revealed this confidence as he wrote to the early believers and reassured them of their value to the Father: "You are a chosen people, a royal priesthood, a holy nation, a people belonging to God" (1 Peter 2:9). The Book of Acts also shows us that this recognition of his identity enabled and empowered Peter's ministry and leadership, endowing him with courage, faithfulness, and a willingness to "go before" others in ministry.

Boldness and courage. Through Peter's example, we see that the leader who is secure in his or her identity as the "beloved of God" will demonstrate boldness and courageous leadership. At the time of Christ's arrest, Peter was afraid of the criticism and accusation of a servant girl. But after Christ had declared his acceptance of and belief in Peter and commissioned him to lead the church, Peter stood unflinchingly against the critics of the early church, facing imprisonment, floggings, and even death. The Book of Acts cites numerous examples of how Peter "stood up" to the crowds to speak about the man named Jesus (Acts 1:15–22; 2:14–41; 3:12–26). He proudly proclaimed his relationship with Christ and boldly appeared before the Sanhedrin to challenge their role in Jesus' death (4:1–22). Peter's courage was also evident as he dealt with the deception of Ananias and Sapphira, thereby protecting the early church by addressing behavior that could have seriously damaged it (5:1–11).

Take a moment to reflect on your identity as the "beloved of God." Then assess the impact that this identity has had on your leadership. Are you confident enough in your identity as a believer in Christ to consistently demonstrate boldness and courage? Are you capable of standing firm in the face of criticism? Are you able to withstand judgment as a leader in the church? Are you willing to proclaim your relationship with Christ unapologetically? Are you equipped to deal with behavior that could hurt the church, or address conflict so that the body of Christ is protected from harm? Only the realization that you truly are the "beloved of God" will enable you to answer "yes" to these questions.

Faith. In addition to being bold, Peter also demonstrated great faith. God, through Peter, healed a crippled beggar, and raised Dorcas from the dead (3:1–10; 9:36–42). In each instance, Peter was careful to acknowledge that he was nothing more than an obedient vessel and that Jesus was the One who had brought the healing.

Take a moment and assess your own leadership. Are you so confident in your relationship with the Lord that you are able to demonstrate great faith? Does your team see your faith in God? Can they see your dependence on Him and your commitment to do what His will entails, even if it looks impossible?

A willingness to "go before" the people. Finally, Peter showed us that leaders who have a secure identity as the "beloved of God" are free to "go before" the people in ministry. Leaders who are confident in their worth rather than performance are able to lead on the "cutting edge," do the unconventional, and share faith-filled vision for how God might work through the lives of His people. Peter demonstrated great leadership as he met with Cornelius and the other Gentiles. Although Jewish law forbade Jews to eat and associate with Gentiles, Peter went to Cornelius' home and stayed several days (Acts 10). Being faith-filled and free from fear, Peter sensed the Holy Spirit leading him to hold tightly to the Gospel message while loosening his grip on traditions and methodologies. He did the unexpected, even the unthinkable, but his actions resulted in the salvation of Gentiles. For the first time in the early church, a relationship with Christ was offered to the rest of the world.

Reflect on your own leadership. Are you confident enough in your worth that you feel free to "go before" the team you serve? Are you prepared to lead on the "cutting edge" and do the unconventional for the sake of the Gospel? Are you willing to set new standards for how God might want to work through you and your team? Are you prepared to manage the healthy tension of remaining faithful to the Gospel while allowing the Holy Spirit to refine some of your methods and traditions?

Experiencing True Fellowship Allows Us to See Ourselves as the Beloved of God.

The Father, through the gift of His Son at Calvary, has declared us worthy of His love, regardless of our performance. Liberty for the relational leader comes from embracing the fullness of this overwhelming grace. God knows that once we come to realize that we are accepted, loved, and valued, a desire to do things consistent with this acceptance, love, and worth will follow. Christ lived out this principle most beautifully when He found Zacchaeus in the top of a sycamore tree. Jesus approached Zacchaeus and offered him friendship and unconditional acceptance. Zacchaeus' livelihood was built on theft, embezzlement, and the betrayal of his people; but Christ showed him that his worth was far greater than his behavior warranted, and this revelation impacted his life in a positive way (Luke 19:1–10).

God is able to give an accurate estimate of our worth because we are created in His image. The coins of Jesus' day bore a picture of Caesar, and only Caesar could declare the money's worth. Only the one whose image was on the coin could determine the value of the coin itself. Likewise, we have been created in the image of God. Each of us was formed according to His great plan and fashioned into a unique individual. Therefore, the Divine Creator has the right to determine our value. He has declared you to be worth the death of His Son—a gift of incomparable value. The One who knew no sin *became* sin and cried out, "My God, My God, why have you forsaken Me?" Why *did* God do it? More important, who did He do it for? He did it for you! You are the beloved of God. If no one else had needed the gift of Calvary, He would have done it for you.

You will now have the opportunity to help each other recognize your common identity as the "beloved of God." You will have the chance to reaffirm one another's worth and value.

Experiencing the Word Together #2

"Let no unwholesome word proceed from your mouth, but only such a word as is good for edification according to the need of the moment, so that it will give grace to those who hear" (Ephesians 4:29 NASB).

Pause now and consider how you might meet one another's need for approval. We define *approval* as "Building up and affirming one another; affirming both the fact of and importance of a relationship." Edification within our fellowship allows the Holy Spirit to confirm through the saints the Father's message of worth to His children. As the Holy Spirit works through us, we are able to minister grace to those who hear. You will now have the opportunity to meet this need of approval for one another and reaffirm the worth of each individual.

Take a moment to think about your partner or each person in your small group. What specific character qualities do you admire in them? What positive character traits have you noticed in each person's life and when have these traits been demonstrated?

Finish this sentence for your partner or each member of your small group.

I have been blessed by your _____. *I saw that when . . .*

(For example: *Karen, I have been blessed by your enthusiasm. I saw that when we worked together with the children in Bible School. You were always excited to see the kids and thrilled by the chance to teach them about God's Word.*)

(For example: *Jim, I have been blessed by your patience. As you have shared about your difficult situation at work, I have been impressed by your acceptance of all that has happened and your willingness to wait on the Lord.*)

Here is a list of other character qualities:

Boldness	Endurance	Initiative
Compassion	Fairness	Loyalty
Contentment	Faith	Responsibility
Creativity	Flexibility	Sensitivity
Determination	Generosity	Sincerity
Diligence	Gentleness	Understanding
Discernment	Gratefulness	Wisdom

Share your words of approval with at least one other person or your small group as directed by your facilitator.

Some of us may have had difficulty receiving the words of approval in the exercise above. We may struggle with our own sense of self-worth. How can we help and challenge one another to see our worth apart from our performance? We must look for opportunities to live out the "Zacchaeus principle" discussed above. We must care for people regardless of their behavior, especially during times of struggle. As we come to know one another and begin to see personal weaknesses or failures, we must seize those opportunities to communicate our acceptance and approval of one another, based on our mutual identity as the beloved of God.

You will now have the opportunity to demonstrate this unconditional love and approval to each other. Christ set the precedent of acceptance. He established the pattern of approval. He gave freely; we received. As we have freely received, we are to freely give (Matthew 10:8).

Experiencing The Word Together #3

"Accept one another, then, just as Christ accepted you, in order to bring praise to God" (Romans 15:7).

Take a moment now and reflect on your own mistakes and failures. Think about a time when you "blew it," disappointed someone, or did something you still feel bad about.

Share that instance of failure now and allow others to give responses that declare your worth apart from your behavior. Experience the Zacchaeus principle with the other participants or members of your team.

I remember sensing/experiencing a time of failure when I . . .

(For example: *I remember sensing a time of failure when I reflected on how little time I gave to our daughter when she was born.*)

As each person shares their time of failure, you will want to respond with words of acceptance and unconditional approval. You will want to accept one another as Christ has accepted you. Those words might sound like. . . .

I know that must have been very difficult for you. It makes me sad to know that you still feel bad about what happened.

It makes me hurt to hear you share that. Yes, that was a mistake, but that's not who you are. It's something you did. I see you as. . . .

Share your responses with another participant or your small group as directed by your leader.

WE GAIN FREEDOM TO BECOME RELATIONAL LEADERS BY LOVING OUR "NEAR ONES."

The third way in which we gain freedom to become relational leaders is by loving our "near ones"—our family members and close friends.

Many Leaders Neglect Their Relationships With Their "Near Ones."

In our misguided attempts to climb the ladders of success, achievement, or notoriety, far too many of us have ignored our relationships with our own family members and closest friends. Somehow we have concluded that it is more important to spend time with co-workers, other ministers, parishioners, or unbelievers than to spend time with those who count the most.

When Jesus gave us the Great Commandment, He combined two Old Testament commandments into one. First, we are to "love the Lord with all our heart, soul and mind." Secondly, we are to "love our neighbor as our self" (see Matthew 22:37–39). This word *neighbor* conveys the meaning "near ones." So in order to live out the Great Commandment of the New Testament, we must love God and love our near ones. If you are married, your spouse is one of your "near ones." If you have children, then your list of "near ones" must include them. If you are a single adult, your "near ones" are your family members and close friends.

God reminds us of this responsibility to love our "near ones" through His Word. Peter exhorts husbands to "be considerate as you live with your wives, and treat them with respect" because the way that a husband loves his wife impacts how God hears his prayers (1 Peter 3:7). The woman of Proverbs 31 is to bring her husband "good, not harm, all the days of her life" so that her husband will have full confidence in her and lack nothing of value. God holds friendships in high esteem as well, as the Bible illustrates through the special intimacy between Jonathan and David (1 Samuel 20:42) and Jesus' fond love for Mary, Martha and Lazarus (John 11:3, 33). Finally, Psalm 127:3 gives us God's perspective on our relationship with our children: "Sons are a heritage from the Lord, children a reward from Him."

The Old Testament provides us with several cautionary examples of leaders who failed to prioritize their "near ones." Their lives bear witness to what happens when we neglect to express our love to those closest to us.

King David missed the opportunity to live out the Great Commandment with his "near ones" by falling victim to temptation and compromise. He sinned against God by committing adultery with Bathsheba, then betrayed his faithful servant Uriah and brought about his death (2 Samuel 11:1–27). Some have observed that if David had gone out to battle (as was the custom of the kings), he might never have fallen into temptation. We could also surmise that if David had simply focused on being a loving husband, he would not have been as vulnerable to the allure of an extramarital affair (2 Samuel 11:1–27). David's tragic fall illustrates the importance of prioritizing the marriage relationship and loving our spouse with Great Commandment love.

Eli failed to embody the Great Commandment in his relationship with his children and experienced the pain and emptiness of misplaced priorities. While he focused upon fulfilling his priestly duties and ministering to the needs of the Israelites, he missed the chance to relate to his own sons. Eli failed to intervene in their lives even when they scorned God's sacrifices and offerings (1 Samuel 2:29). He admitted that others seemed to know more about his sons than he did (v. 23). The life of Eli offers sobering proof of the importance of prioritizing our relationships with our children and loving them with Great Commandment love. To those in leadership, it might be helpful to consider a paraphrased application of Christ's warning in Matthew 16:26. What good will it be for you if you gain the whole world and lose your family?

As We Love Our "Near Ones," Our Leadership Is Positively Impacted.

"A new command I give you: Love one another. As I have loved you, so you must love one another. By this all men will know that you are my disciples, if you love one another" (John 13:34, 35).

Jesus wanted His disciples to understand that a heart of love must be the defining evidence of someone who follows Christ. He gave them this new commandment to love one another as a clear indication of what they were to prioritize as they began to lead the church. The disciples had actually shown evidence of this kind of love at the very beginning of their relationship with Jesus. The New Testament tells us that Andrew introduced Jesus to his brother, Simon Peter (1:40–42) and that Philip shared the news about Jesus with his friend Nathanael (v. 45). We also see the disciples' collective commitment to loving their families in the account of Peter's mother-in-law. Scripture reveals that it was "they" who "told Jesus about her" (Mark 1:30). The disciples were confident that the Lord would want them to give attention to the need of this hurting family member.

The disciples' understanding of the concept of loving "near ones" increased as they saw Jesus model this same commitment. As He hung on the cross, Jesus gave John instructions to care for His mother in His absence (John 19:27). Throughout His ministry, Jesus also took time to love and serve His twelve companions, a fact that is most clearly illustrated by His last night with them before His death: "Jesus knew that the Father had put all things under his power, and that he had come from God and was returning to God . . . he poured water into a basin and began to wash his disciples' feet" (13:3, 5).

> **Relational leaders must first love God and then lovingly invest in their spouses, children, family members, and close friends.**

After washing His disciples' feet, Jesus encouraged them to love and serve one another: "Now that I, your Lord and Teacher, have washed your feet, you also should wash one another's feet. I have set you an example that you should do as I have done for you" (vv. 14, 15). Jesus promised that as the disciples gave care to their "near ones," they would be blessed: "Now that you know these things, you will be blessed if you do them" (v. 17). Likewise, relational leaders must make it their priority to first love God, and then to lovingly invest in their spouses, children, family members, and close friends.

Experiencing True Fellowship Encourages Us to Love Our "Near Ones."

"Let us consider how to stimulate one another to love and good deeds" (Hebrews 10:24 NASB).

This passage in Hebrews reminds us that we all need to be encouraged to love one another. We also need to be held accountable for how we are living out the Great Commandment in our relationships. Our fellowship with one another provides the ideal context in which to do just that. As we gather together in our small groups, Bible studies, or mentoring relationships, a portion of our time should be devoted to giving an account of how well we are loving our "near ones." In our times of fellowship, we must purposefully stimulate one another toward loving our family members and close friends.

If you are married, you might address these questions in your times of fellowship:

- What have we recently done as a couple, just for fun?
- How are we doing at finding uninterrupted, focused time together?
- Are those times drawing us closer?

- What demonstrations of my loving initiative have recently brought expressions of gratitude from my spouse?

If you have children, you might address these questions in your times of fellowship:

- What have we recently done as a family, just for fun?
- How are we doing at finding focused time with each individual child?
- Are those times drawing us closer?
- When have we recently shown verbalized love, interest, and involvement in our children's activities and care for their joys and pain?

If you are unmarried and without children, you might address these questions in your times of fellowship:

- What have I recently done with family members or close friends, just for fun?
- How am I doing at finding focused time with family members and friends? Are those times drawing us closer?
- When have I recently shown verbalized love, interest, and involvement in another's activities and care for their joys and pain?

As we have mentioned in previous chapters, it will not be our own determination or willpower that will sustain our efforts to love our "near ones." The empowerment to love will only come as the Holy Spirit works in our lives, transforming us into the image of Christ. Take a few moments now and reflect on Christ's heart for your "near ones."

Experiencing the Word Together #4

"Take my yoke upon you and learn of me, for I am gentle and humble" (Matthew 11:29).

Imagine Christ standing before you in flowing robes, with sandaled feet. He has a bearded face and nail-pierced hands. His eyes are kind and gentle. His expression is loving, yet somehow sad. As you look more closely, you notice that Christ is wearing a yoke—a yoke of service and love. The purpose of this yoke is to allow One who is experienced to train another. Jesus stands before you wearing the yoke, but the other side of the yoke is empty. There is no one to share the special calling to love your "near ones." There is no one to share the unique task of caring for those closest to you. You begin to realize that Jesus has been serving your loved ones, but He has often been serving them alone. Christ has been ministering to the people around you, but He has often been ministering without you.

Listen to His words again: "Take my yoke upon you and learn of me." Now consider those nearest you—your spouse, children, other family members, and friends. Recognize the fact that Christ is constantly taking thought of them, encouraging them, and comforting them when they are hurting, but He may be doing those things without you. He often loves your nearest ones alone.

Listen as Jesus whispers to you: "Come take the other side of this yoke and together we can love your near ones well! Come to Me and learn what I know about those nearest you. Learn how to lavish them with love. Come join Me in the yoke and find that you have been joined to the One who *is* love.

Pause now and pray with one another, yielding yourself and committing to join Christ in loving those nearest you.

"Lord Jesus, I do want to join You in better loving_____. I yield myself to learn from You how to love them well. Change me, Gentle Teacher, as I am yoked with You."

Take a few moments now and live out the admonishment of Hebrews 10:24. Begin to stimulate one another to love and good deeds. Encourage one another to live out the Great Commandment with your "near ones." You can do this by vulnerably sharing whom God might want to love through you. Whom will you join Him in loving?

I believe God might want to love _____ *through my . . .*

I believe God might want to love _____ *through my . . .*

For example: *I believe God might want to love my wife through my attentive care and my commitment to become more emotionally attuned to her needs.*

For example: *I believe God might want to love my friend David through my acceptance of him and concern for his struggles.*

Complete these sentences and share your responses with your partner or small group as directed by your facilitator. Then pray for one another, asking the Spirit to empower each person to be a co-laborer with Christ.

Chapter 5 Outline

I. **We Gain Freedom to Become Relational Leaders by Having an Accurate View of God.**

   A. How Do You View God?

   Personal Exercise #1 and **My Team Journal #1**

   B. Our View of God Can Impact Our Leadership.

      1. The Example of King Saul

         a. What poor decisions did he make?

            (1) 1 Samuel 13:7–14

            (2) 1 Samuel 15:1–23

         b. How did he treat people?

            (1) His son Jonathan (1 Samuel 14:24–30; 43–45)

            (2) David (1 Samuel 18:7–11; 19:9–16)

            (3) Himself (1 Samuel 31:1–6)

         c. How might his view of God have affected both his decision-making and the way he treated people?

      2. The Example of King David

         a. His decision to fight Goliath (1 Samuel 17:37)

         b. His decision to serve Saul in spite of threats to his life (1 Samuel 24:9–13)

   C. Hindered Views of God

      1. Inspecting

      2. Disappointed

      3. Distant

   Personal Exercise #2 and **My Team Journal #2**

D. Experiencing True Fellowship Allows Us to See the Real God.

    1. "No one has ever seen God. But if we love each other, God lives in us, and his love has been brought to full expression through us" (1 John 4:12 NLT).

    2. Loving each other changes our concept of God—we see Him as He really is:

        a. When someone fails, and we accept them (Romans 15:7)

        b. When someone struggles, and we encourage them (Hebrews 10:25)

        c. When someone hurts, and we comfort them (2 Corinthians 1:3, 4)

Experiencing the Word Together #1

II. We Gain Freedom to Become Relational Leaders by Embracing Our Identity as the Beloved of God.

A. How Do We Define Our Value and Worth?

    1. Do I equate "what I do" with "who I am"?

        a. Am I driven to "do more" in order to feel better about myself?

        b. Am I critical of others and myself?

        c. Am I overly sensitive and defensive, particularly in response to feedback concerning my performance?

    2. God separates our worth from our performance.

        a. The example of Peter

           (1) He failed Jesus terribly.

           (2) Yet Jesus restored him to relationship and to leadership (John 21).

        b. For us: "God demonstrates his own love for us in this: While we were still sinners, Christ died for us" (Romans 5:8).

           (1) He has blessed us with every spiritual blessing (Ephesians 1:3).

           (2) He chose us (v. 4).

           (3) He adopted us as sons and daughters (v. 5).

           (4) He has freely given us his glorious grace (v. 6).

(5) He has redeemed and forgiven us, according to the riches of his grace lavished upon us (v. 7, 8).

(6) All because He wanted to: "In accordance with his pleasure and will . . . according to his good pleasure" (v. 5, 9).

B. The Fruit of Being Secure in Our Identity

1. Boldness and courage in the face of opposition and persecution

   a. The example of Peter (Acts 2:14–41; 3:12–26)

   b. Are we confident enough in God's love to be consistently bold and courageous?

2. Great faith

   a. The example of Peter (Acts 3:1–10; 9:36-42)

   b. Are we secure enough in our identity as the beloved of God to demonstrate great faith?

3. A willingness to "go before" the people with cutting edge vision and initiatives

   a. The example of Peter (Acts 10)

   b. Are we confident enough of our infinite worth to God that we can "go before" the people with fresh (possibly risky) vision and initiatives?

C. Experiencing True Fellowship Allows Us to See Ourselves as the Beloved of God.

Experiencing the Word Together #2

Experiencing the Word Together #3

III. **We Gain Freedom to Become Relational Leaders by Loving Our "Near Ones."**

A. Many Leaders Neglect Their Relationships With Their "Near Ones."

1. Scripture affirms the importance of caring for our "near ones," both family and friends (Ephesians 5:22–33, I Peter 3:1–7, Proverbs 31:10–31, Psalm 127:3, 1 Timothy 5:8, Proverbs 17:17).

2. David failed to prioritize his family and fell into great sin (2 Samuel 11).

3. Eli failed to be involved with and discipline his sons, with disastrous results (1 Samuel 2:12-36; 4:1–22).

B. As We Love Our "Near Ones," Our Leadership is Positively Impacted.

1. Others will know that we are his disciples if we love one another (John 13:35).

2. What good would it be if you gained the whole world, but lost your family?

C. Experiencing True Fellowship Encourages Us to Love Our "Near Ones."

1. "Let us consider how we may spur one another on toward love" (Hebrews 10:24).

2. Ask questions to assess your care for your "near ones."

a. Married Couples—What have we recently done as a couple for fun? Are we spending regular, uninterrupted, focused time together for planning, calendaring, and appreciating each other? Are we experiencing meaningful times with the Lord together in worship, scripture study, and prayer? Do we demonstrate loving initiative toward one another?

b. Parents—What have we done recently together for fun? Are we spending individual time with each child? Are those times drawing us closer? When have we recently verbalized love, shown interest in a child's activities, and expressed care for their joys and pains?

c. As brothers and sisters in Christ—What have we done recently just for fun with those outside of our immediate family? Are we consistently sharing our lives with each other in ways that draw us closer to one another? When have we recently verbalized love, shown interest in another's activities, and expressed care for others' joys and pains?

Experiencing the Word Together #4

Additional Resources

Henry T. Blackaby and Claude V. King, *Experiencing God* (Nashville: Broadman & Holman Publishers, 1998).

Jim Collins, *Good to Great* (New York: HarperCollins, 2001).

Jerry W. Gilley and Nathaniel W. Boughton, *Stop Managing, Start Coaching*! (New York: McGraw-Hill, 1995).

Robert E. Quinn, *Deep Change: Discovering the Leader Within* (San Francisco: Jossey-Bass Inc., 1996).

Charles R. Swindoll, *The Grace Awakening* (Dallas: Word Publishing, 1996).

Chapter 6

Relational Vision: Focusing Together on Eternal Priorities

As we experience genuine fellowship with one another, our misconceptions of God are challenged and we are encouraged to leave behind our performance-based sense of worth and our misplaced priorities. As these hindrances are removed from our lives and our leadership, we receive freedom to love and serve others (Galatians 5:13). Throughout this chapter and the next, we will discuss the third part of our definition of relational leadership, namely accomplishing significant and lasting objectives. Our fellowship together must begin with the Spirit's deepened work in us as individuals and as a team, but it must not stop there. True *koinonia* also involves partnering together for God's kingdom, and making contributions toward fulfilling the Great Commission to make disciples of all nations. Once we, as relational leaders, have encouraged our teams to develop hearts of servanthood, promoted an atmosphere of mutual care, and left behind those things that hinder effective leadership, we are then ready to partner together in this aspect of divine calling. Within this atmosphere of caring connectedness and genuine fellowship, we are better able to discern the vision of God, His call upon our lives, and His plan for our team.

How would you define *vision*? In the context of leadership, vision involves imagining what could happen, thus producing a mental picture of what the future might look like. According to business consultant Dennis Perkins, an effective vision will address long-term strategies and large-scale objectives, as well as providing the means to consistently achieve the critical short-term goals which help to sustain momentum and ensure survival (Perkins, 2000). We must maintain this dual focus on "the big picture" and the day-to-day details if we are to discern vision that will lead to increased spiritual health and growth in both our personal lives and our ministries.

Take a moment now to reflect on the questions below. Think about how you might answer these questions independently and then brainstorm with your team or partner:

- What are three critical short-term challenges or obstacles that you are currently facing in your personal life or ministry? How might you go about addressing these issues?
- Can you list three long-term personal goals?
- Can you identify three long-term ministry goals for your team?
- How do your personal and ministry visions relate to Christ's Great Commission to "go forth and make disciples"?

You may want to record these responses in the Team Journal at the end of the chapter.

The extent to which you were able to answer the questions above may reflect the clarity of your personal or team vision. These questions may also have served to broaden your view of vision-casting and how it might relate to fellowship with one another.

As some of you discussed the issues related to vision, you may have asked yourselves, "How can we know what God wants for our lives? How can we gain an understanding of His plans for our team?" As relational leaders, we must come to understand the fundamentals of discerning vision.

THE FUNDAMENTALS OF DISCERNING VISION: THREE GOD-CENTERED QUESTIONS

"Where there is no vision, the people are unrestrained" (Proverbs 29:18 NASB).

All of us need vision. Without it, our jobs and ministries can become routine obligation or even mindless drudgery. In order to avoid such an unfulfilling environment for ourselves and our team, it is essential that we trust the Spirit of God to give us a vision for that which is lasting and eternal. In order to discern vision that is consistent with the heart of God, relational leaders must learn to ask God-centered questions.

> **Relational leaders must begin the vision-discernment process by asking God-centered questions.**

Where Is God Leading?

As relational leaders begin to develop a vision for their teams, they must first consider the question, "Where is God leading?" Vision must begin with the One who has the plans for our future and our hope (Jeremiah 29:11 NASB).

As we begin the process of discerning vision, we must spend quiet, uninterrupted time with God, allowing Him to give us insight and confirmation of His plans, His hopes, and His agenda. We must "be still" in order for God to reveal His direction (Psalm 46:10). As we spend time coming to know God and having fellowship with Him, we will be better able to discern where God wants to take us, and more convinced that He is fully capable of taking us there.

In order for this question to truly be a God-centered one, however, we must ask it with the proper emphasis—not just "**Where** is God leading?" but "Where is **God** leading?" When we focus too much on the "where," we often end up asking a completely different question, namely "Where do **we want** God to lead us?"

Focusing on God's leading allows relational leaders to resist the pull of "man-centered" goals that are driven by earthly concerns or derived in response to the approval of people. We indeed live and minister "in the world," but our approach and priorities must be "not of the world" (John 17:11, 16).

All of us have, at times, devised and carried out our own vision, only to later entreat God for His blessing and provision, almost as an afterthought. Some of those plans are graciously blessed and others fail, but we must realize that regardless of the outcome, the point of origin was wrong. The idea, vision, or goal originated with us—not Him! This principle of origin must guide relational leaders in discerning personal and team vision. We must be cautious about making plans based upon man's ideas, fears, needs, or values. Rather, man's concerns must be brought before the Lord in order to better sense His desires and His direction. Relational leaders must consider the question, "Was the origin of this idea, plan, goal, or vision man's flesh or God's Spirit?"

Personal Exercise #1

I recall the pain of being affected by one of man's visions for . . .

(For example: *I recall the pain of being affected by one of man's visions for church assimilation. The instructors meant well, but the class was intimidating and uncomfortable. It definitely did not make me want to "plug into" the church in any meaningful way.*)

Why Would God Lead Us There?

As leaders begin to develop a vision for their team and start to sense where God is leading, they must next ask, "Why would God lead us there?" It is not enough to simply ask for God's direction. We must also strive to understand the heart and motive behind the vision He reveals.

All too often, leaders are content to see God "opening doors" and producing results, and they fail to ask "Why?" They miss out on gaining greater insight into the heart of God, to their own detriment. The Israelites fell into this same trap during their wilderness wanderings. Psalm 103:7 tells us that Moses knew the "ways of God," but the children of Israel only saw the "deeds of God." Our goal is to know God and His ways. We must not be content with simply seeing His acts, no matter how spectacular or miraculous.

Personal Exercise #2

As I imagine God revealing His ways to me, I . . .

(For example: *As I imagine God revealing His ways to me, I am excited about the possibility of such a close relationship with the Lord and how that would impact my certainty of vision and direction.*)

As relational leaders discern the answers to the two questions above, they must begin the process of casting the vision before the team. As a leader carefully articulates where God seems to be leading and why He might be leading in that direction, ownership for the vision grows. The vision thus becomes an opportunity for **us** to bless the Lord rather than focusing on **me** and **my** agenda. In this way, leaders are able to guard against trying to "sell" their team on where they should go and why they should go there.

Does Our Vision Reflect Concern for Eternal Things?

As we pursue this task of communicating vision to our teams, it is important to note the above emphasis on where God **seems** to be leading and why He **might** be leading there. An effective leader will come to their team with a sense of discernment that is held lightly, allowing the Spirit to refine, enhance, and confirm the vision. As the Spirit brings clarity, we must consider a third God-centered question: "Does our vision reflect concern for eternal things?"

> **A vision that is divinely confirmed will be based on eternal things— God, His Word, and people.**

God will only lead us toward a vision that is concerned with things that last, things that will exist for all of eternity. Therefore, a vision that is divinely confirmed will be based on God, His Word, and people.

Think about all of your planning, all the events, activities, and programs. How many of these things will last forever? How many of your meetings, discussions, and promotions relate to eternity? The sobering conclusion for many of us is that often very little of what we do in the name of ministry will stand the test of time. But relational leaders are committed to a different set of priorities. They ask the Spirit to redirect any plans that do not reflect God's eternal priorities, knowing that only a vision based on things eternal will be "of the Lord" and blessed abundantly by Him.

Does our vision bring glory and honor to the Eternal One? We know that God is eternal. He "was" before time began and "will be" for all of time in the future. Our worship, our praise, and our prayers to Him are all significant because they are directed toward One who is eternal and will last forever. If we are indeed convinced that He is worthy of our glory and honor, then all of our plans, discussions, and goals must always have Him as a reference point. Only a vision that brings God praise and honor, one that gives us the opportunity to say, "Look what God has done!" is worthy of your team's efforts.

King Solomon was a mighty leader with a tender heart. At first glance, it would be easy to conclude that he wanted to build the greatest temple in Jewish history in order to create a legacy of honor and personal fame. We know from Scripture, however, that that was not his goal. Solomon's heartfelt prayer was for "a discerning heart to govern your people and to distinguish between right and wrong" (1 Kings 3:9). He envisioned the great temple as a way to bring glory and honor to God.

Relational leaders must be able to answer the same question: "How will our vision bring glory and honor to the Lord?" Is He pleased by our agenda and blessed by the motives of our heart? Do our discussions of buildings, programs, and promotions serve a greater, eternal purpose that honors Him, or do they stop with only the temporal? How do the color of the carpet, committee assignments, and choir specials relate to His glory? As leaders continue the process of discerning vision, they challenge others to consider how future plans would please, bless, and honor the Eternal One. Then with a spirit of humility, they lead by example, redirecting discussions as necessary to prayerfully, purposefully consider the Lord.

Personal Exercise #3

Refer back to one of your personal or team goals and reflect on the following:

God would be blessed and honored as we address _____ since He . . .

(For example: *God would be blessed and honored as we address the need for ongoing marriage ministry in our church, since He is concerned about marriages and how well we are able to demonstrate love to one another. He would also be pleased to see our efforts to make this marriage class an outreach opportunity that draws people to Him.*)

Does our vision align with the eternal Word of God? Just as God is eternal, so is His Word. The Scriptures tell us that "the grass withers and the flowers fall, but the word of our God stands forever" (Isaiah 40:8). A God-inspired vision will be built around an understanding of the eternal significance of the Word. Relational leaders must be able to see that their vision clearly aligns with God's Word, and must reject any plans, ideas, or goals that violate Scripture.

Since the implementation of an effective vision requires not only God's direction, but also a certain measure of relational connectedness, the entire process of vision development must align with the Word of God. As we begin to define details of a vision and discuss its implications, all of our words, actions, and attitudes must be governed by scriptural principles. God's multi-faceted love, as expressed in 1 Corinthians 13, must be exemplified in our interactions as we make plans with our team. The wisdom of Proverbs and lessons from Israel and the first-century church must be drawn upon as we set goals for ministry. We must always be able to see evidence of the "one anothers" of Scripture being lived out among His people. We must accept one another, encourage one another, and build up one another with our words (Romans 15:7; 1 Thessalonians 5:11; Ephesians 4:29). Without a commitment to live out God's Word as we discern and implement His vision, our plans will not accomplish all that we hope. Even the greatest vision will be lost or impaired if we violate God's principles while striving to develop it.

Finally, whether we are measuring our interactions with one another against scriptural principles or evaluating the eternal merits of a vision as a whole, the Holy Spirit will give validation, confirmation, and direction as God's Word is illuminated. Peter's declaration concerning the birth of the church in Acts 2:16 is an example of this. As Peter referred to all that was taking place on the Day of Pentecost, he declared, "This is what was spoken by the prophet Joel." Peter recognized that Joel 2:28—"I will pour out my spirit on all people"— was being fulfilled in their midst. Relational leaders must look for this same evidence in both the process and implementation of their vision. They must be able to say, "This is 'that.' This vision is evidence of God's Word being lived out by His people."

Personal Exercise #4

Refer back to one of your personal or team challenges or goals and reflect on the following:

As I/we address _____, it seems important to consider Scripture's direction concerning . . .
(Refer to specific Scripture passages as much as possible.)

(For example: *As we address the possibility of establishing an ongoing marriage ministry in our church, it seems important to consider Scripture's direction concerning marriage relationships. Are we training our husbands to live with their wives in an understanding way* (1 Peter 3:7 NASB)? *Are we training our wives to live so that their husbands trust them, have full confidence in them, and lack nothing of value* (Proverbs 31:11)? *Have the couples in our church received adequate training and opportunity to live these principles out with one another?*)

Does our vision positively impact people, who are eternal? Just as God and His Word will last forever, so will those whom He has created. People have an eternal destiny. Therefore, when we discuss vision among our team, we must always consider how our vision will affect and positively impact the ones whom God has declared worth the gift of His Son. Leaders must consider what God wants for His children, the "household of faith" (see Ephesians 2:19). They must ask, "What can we envision for the people we have been called to serve? What would God desire for His chosen ones?" These questions challenge us to begin with people in mind. We must filter all our discussions, decisions, actions, and recommendations through the question, "How will people be served?" As we seek to implement vision with people as a priority, we should remember that Christ continued to serve people until the very end, declaring that "I am among you as one who serves" (Luke 22:27). Likewise, our service is not to be merely a function of the job we hold. We must be motivated first and foremost by sincere love for people. God's love for people is demonstrated throughout Scripture, but especially by His desire "that all should come to repentance" (2 Peter 3:9 KJV). Our vision must be shaped by a recognition of God's longing for people to be reconciled to Him, by the realization that His Spirit actively convicts us (John 16:8–11), and by the knowledge that Christ is ever living to make intercession for us (Hebrews 7:25). God deeply desires that people would come to know Him, the only true God, and Jesus Christ whom He sent (John 17:3). We, as leaders and members of His church, must be motivated by this same passion for people.

Vision at any level has stopped too short unless it is brought into alignment with God's desire that others know Him. The more we submit to God's guidance and direction, the more we will come to sense His loving heart and burden for those who do not know Him. As we discern where God is leading and what vision He is birthing among us, we must ask ourselves, "Will our decisions, actions, programs, and promotions enhance (and not hinder) our testimony of Christ to a needy world?"

MOVING FROM INDIVIDUAL VISION TO RELATIONAL VISION

"Why do . . . all these people stand around you from morning till evening?" (Exodus 18:14).

This insightful Old Testament passage raises significant questions for today's church and its leaders. Why do so many "stand around"? We know that demands on people's time are challenging and that their motivation sometimes seems lacking. It is undeniable that the commitment level of many church members is low and that feelings of apathy toward a lost world are rampant. But there may be a more serious underlying problem. Is it possible that many of those around us simply hear about "our" burdens, "our" goals, and "our" plans for the church, without the vision ever becoming truly **our** vision? Even if we have discerned a vision we feel quite sure is from God and reflects His concern for eternal priorities, it is doomed to fail if it is not shared by others. We need a relational vision—a vision that is shared by our team and that is developed out of our relationships with one another.

Typical Vision-Development Process

> **God-centered vision must be discerned and developed within the context of relationships.**

In a typical vision-development process, leaders tend to gravitate to one of two extremes. At one extreme, the leader has all of the vision and seems only to announce that vision to his or her team. Plans, ideas, and goals are simply imposed upon those whom the vision is supposed to inspire. The crucial step of seeking to involve others in the process of discerning vision is simply omitted. Those who attempt to lead in this way fail to realize that no vision can be accomplished by one person's edict.

At the second extreme, team members wait around for someone else to "come up with" a vision. Too often, large segments of a church body are content with being spectators or, at best, limited participants in someone else's vision. This lack of involvement on the part of the congregation is a critical factor in explaining why too few actually become "equipped saints" for the work of the ministry (Ephesians 4:12 NASB).

Typical Vision-Development Process

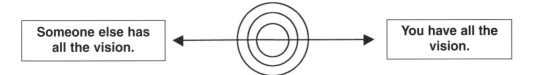

Relational Vision-Development Process
Relational leaders reject this typical process in favor of a relational approach to vision-development. In this approach, leaders are first served with vision as they receive from God and from others. Team members then make contributions to the vision, and finally, others' vision is incorporated.

Relational Vision-Development Process

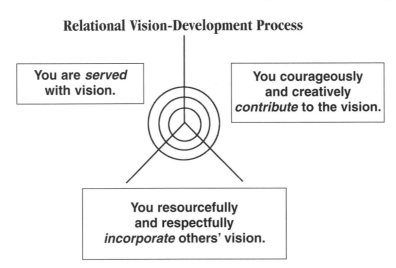

Before we begin our specific description of relational vision, consider as a frame of reference Christ's words to the apostles and others in Acts 1:8: "But you will receive power . . . you will be my witnesses in Jerusalem, and in all Judea and Samaria, and to the ends of the earth." Notice that Christ did not prescribe exactly who would do what in the church, but left that to be determined later as the apostles walked with Him and with one another. After the Spirit's coming at Pentecost, Peter, James, John, and others contributed their part of the vision in the Jerusalem church, in Samaria, and in the home of Cornelius. Others, such as Philip, Stephen, Aquila, Priscilla, and Lydia, added their part to the vision.

Then Saul of Tarsus, later renamed Paul, was led to incorporate his burden for Christ's Great Commission, even challenging Peter and the others at the Jerusalem council to refine and refocus God's vision for His church (Acts 15). The vision did not change in content or in focus. They were still to be Christ's witnesses to the rest of the world. But the vision grew more well-defined and was more broadly embraced at each stage of the process.

In a similar way, as we begin the process of discovering the vision God has for us, we must remember that as we involve other people in the vision, some changes may occur. The vision may be refined or further developed. But more importantly, as we involve other people, the vision will become more broadly embraced.

Read the descriptions of each stage in the relational vision-development process and then work through the Personal Exercises in order to begin your own vision discovery process.

You are served with vision. Janna was inspired to begin the ministry of *Rebecca's House* by her own life experiences and her gratefulness for what God had done. She began to sense God's vision for her life as God brought her in contact with numerous young girls who were in the midst of crisis pregnancies. The fact that Janna came from a similar background made it easy for her to care for these girls. Her heart of compassion and practical support drew the girls to a relationship with Christ. God revealed to Janna a vision for a ministry to unwed mothers, one that she was uniquely suited to lead because of her own experiences. Janna's reflection on Romans 8:28 gave her the sense that God wanted to bring good out of her life's journey, that He wanted to develop in her a heart of compassion and a burden to help others.

Finally, God confirmed the vision for *Rebecca's House* when He brought together a team of ladies who had been impacted by Janna's life and who, out of their own gratefulness, wanted to partner together in ministry. Their gifts of time, energy, and resources made it clear that Janna was pursuing a vision that was blessed by God.

Just as the vision for Janna's life was confirmed by God, we can also receive assurance of God's direction for us. Since He will always lead toward lasting objectives, we must constantly filter our vision through the grid of eternal priorities. Take a moment now and reflect on how God might have served you with a vision for your life and ministry.

Personal Exercise #5

Being Served With Vision

Relational leaders are served with vision by spending time with God, His Word, and other people. As you consider where God might be leading you or your team, you will need to examine each source of insight.

If you are working through this exercise with your ministry team, you may want to reflect on some of the challenges or issues discussed during your brainstorming time at the beginning of this session. You and your team will then approach these exercises with one particular challenge or obstacle in mind.

If you are working through this exercise with a partner, you may want to complete your vision planning/discovery in a more general way as detailed in the exercise.

I am served with vision through my time with God.
1. Spend time in prayer. Ask the Holy Spirit to give you direction and to show you His desires for you or your team. Pray that you would receive all that He has to tell you. Pray specifically about the following:

God, what do You want for us? What do You want to show me concerning Your vision for my life and our ministry?

God, please bring to mind a few key events that have shaped my life, burden, calling, or vision for ministry.

You may have a sense of where God is leading and how He has confirmed His vision for you up to this point. Reflect on what God may have already revealed to you.

God, as I have spent time with You, I sense that You might want me to . . .

God, as I have spent time with You and reflected upon my life experiences, specifically concerning _____, *I sense that You might desire . . .*

I am served with vision through God's Word.
2. Spend time in God's Word. Search for confirmation of a vision by the Scriptures.

First, reflect on how has God given you direction through His Word on previous occasions. How has He revealed His plans for you through Scripture? Are there any particular "life verses" that have shaped your experiences?

In the past, God's leading in my life was confirmed by His Word in some of the following verses . . .

Next, reflect on how God might have given you direction recently in the Scriptures.

After recently spending time in God's Word, a particular Scripture verse that God might want me to consider is . . .

I am served with vision through the contributions of others.
3. Give consideration to the directives, input, or guidance of others that may shape your ministry vision.

I/we have been served with a measure of vision by _____, *who shared . . .*

Reflect on how God might have spoken to you through other people. How might He have allowed others to share His vision with you? Have others confirmed particular gifts in you? Affirmed your burden or calling in a specific area? Shared a possible direction for ministry and given you an opportunity to pursue it?

I sense that God affirmed me and my gifts or abilities through _____ *when . . .*

After all three steps have been completed, summarize the sense of vision you have received to this point: express your vision in writing, including references to important life events, Scripture verses, and confirmation through other people. Share your reflections with your partner or small group. You may want to record these responses in the Team Journal at the end of the chapter.

Where is God leading?
God seems to be leading me/us . . .

Why would He lead us there?
As He leads us in these ways, He would receive glory through . . .

You courageously and creatively contribute to the vision. Al and Jan have recently returned from a church leadership retreat where the senior pastor led the staff in a vision-casting and planning session. As a result of the pastor's shared vision and a corporate prayer time, the entire staff sensed a new passion from the Lord about the church's outreach and community involvement. Al and Jan listened to the pastor express his heart and felt a similar burden to extend their ministry to the families who live near their church campus. As the associate pastor, Al has now been served with a vision for the church and is being challenged to contribute to that vision. He and Jan have often discussed how wonderful it would be to offer "no cost" family nights for people in the neighborhood. They have brainstormed about ways to finance such a ministry and discussed creative ideas for helping these events translate to ongoing ministry. Al and Jan have wondered if God might be able to work through Al's sales and marketing background and Jan's giftedness in assimilation. They have decided to pray about the opportunities and challenges that an outreach ministry might present and to actively look for ways that they might live out the church's new passion to reach unbelievers.

Just as each of us may be called upon to serve one another with vision, each of us, at times, will be called upon to courageously contribute vision to help refine and confirm God's leading. Since God has not given us a spirit of fear (2 Timothy 1:7 KJV), we can share with great certainty about His leading in our lives. Your creativity in contributing to the vision comes through the Holy Spirit's unique leading and gifting in your life. God has so composed the body that we need one another and the special perspective and calling we each bring (1 Corinthians 12:21–27).

Personal Exercise #6

Courageously and Creatively Contributing to the Vision

If you are working through this exercise with your ministry team, you may want to continue to pursue vision for one of the challenges or obstacles discussed in your brainstorming session. If you are working through this exercise with a partner, you may want to complete this exercise with one of your existing ministry goals in mind.

I contribute to a vision after spending time with God.

1. Spend time in prayer, asking God to reveal how you might contribute to the vision you have received. Ask Him to show you how you might strengthen the vision, bring more impact, or extend the vision for His glory. Your prayer might include . . .

Lord, how can I contribute to the vision through my gifts, talents, and callings so as to bring more positive impact for the cause of Christ?

God, please show me how You have prepared me through my life experiences to make contributions to this vision.

After spending time in prayer, I sense that God might want me to contribute to the vision in the following ways . . .

I contribute to a vision after spending time in God's Word.

2. Spend time in God's Word, seeking out the scriptural principles and passages that relate to your contributions to the vision you have received. Ask for God to confirm through His Word how you might add to the vision. In your search through the Scriptures, you might consider . . .

Are there specific passages of Scripture that seem applicable to the vision?

Are there any "cautions" from Scripture that seem appropriate?

Does the vision violate or oppose Scripture in any way?

Has God impressed me through His Word and given me specific ideas about how I might contribute?

After spending time in God's Word, I sense that God might want me to contribute to the vision in the following ways . . .

I contribute to a vision after spending time with God's people.
3. Spend time reflecting upon how your contributions might be confirmed or needed by other people. Realize that the vision will be incomplete without your input. Your contribution to the ministry is uniquely your own. Reflect on these questions as you finalize your ideas for how you might add value or impact to a vision that you have received:

How has God spoken to me through the confirmation of His people and validated my contribution to this vision? What would "my piece" of this vision look like?

After spending time with God's people, I sense that God might want me to contribute to the vision in the following ways . . .

As you complete the three steps above, summarize your ideas about how you might contribute to the vision. Be ready to share these reflections with your team and/or leader. Be sure to share with a spirit of servanthood and humility, guarding against defensiveness when others have a different perspective than yours. Share your responses with your team or partner. You may want to record these responses in the Team Journal at the end of the chapter.

I sense that God might want me to contribute to the vision in the following ways . . .

I sense that God might want me to take responsibility in . . .

Specific Scripture verses that seem applicable include . . .

You respectfully and resourcefully incorporate others' vision. Larry and Sharon have recently discovered a part of the vision they sense God has for them and their adult Bible class. They first took their vision to the pastoral staff member who oversees the class. Larry discussed their growing sense that God might want them to divide their existing Bible class into two separate entities. One class would serve as an ongoing ministry to married couples within the church, while the other would focus on curriculum designed to address the needs of couples in crisis. Having both classes available would provide opportunities for the study of God's Word in an environment with others who are in a similar life-stage, but also meet the immediate needs of couples struggling in their marriage.

Larry and Sharon were excited to hear the staff member's contributions to the vision and sensed God's confirmation upon their plans for the class. The staff member suggested creative ways to let both church members and the unchurched families in the neighborhood know about each of the classes. Next, Larry and Sharon shared the vision they believed God had given them with other lay leaders of their class, hoping to hear contributions from these individuals as well. God once again confirmed their direction. Two couples volunteered to step in and continue the ongoing Bible study so that Larry and Sharon would be free to begin the class for hurting marriages.

As the process continued, Larry and Sharon worked diligently to incorporate the vision of other members of their class. Class members gave input that was helpful in delineating the structure of each class, creating effective promotions, and assisting with the inevitable administrative issues. Larry and Sharon were truly blessed by the process of developing a relational vision. Their excitement grew each step of the way as God refined and enhanced the vision for their ministry.

In order for vision to become shared and "owned" by others, it is important to include as many other people as possible in the discovery of the vision. The writer of Proverbs reminds us that "with many advisers [plans] succeed" (Proverbs 15:22). As we follow the relational vision process, we may see God involve a variety of people in numerous roles. Since relational leaders are always mindful of the benefit of multiple counselors, they see the opportunity to involve others as a blessing rather than an inconvenience.

What might this process look like in a local church setting? One possible scenario is for pastoral leadership to be served vision from church elders, overseers, or others in leadership.

The pastoral team members then courageously and creatively contribute their gifts, callings, and abilities to the vision and finally are ready to respectfully and resourcefully incorporate others' vision. Pastoral leadership might seek out key lay leaders, deacons, or the church council to get input and feedback about the vision.

At another time, the pastoral leadership might serve vision to lay leaders who oversee adult, youth, or children's ministries. These lay leaders would then creatively and courageously contribute their vision, and respectfully and resourcefully incorporate vision from the adult, youth, and children's teachers. The teachers might in turn communicate vision to those they serve, enlist members' input, and in some cases even devise ways to receive feedback from the unchurched of their community.

Take a moment now and reflect on how you might continue the discovery of a relational vision. Consider how you can begin to respectfully and resourcefully incorporate the vision of others.

Personal Exercise #7

Respectfully and Resourcefully Incorporating Others' Vision

As you consider how you might incorporate others' vision, follow these important steps:

I can better incorporate others' contributions to our vision after spending time with God.

1. Spend time in prayer, asking God to show you how to respectfully and resourcefully incorporate others' vision. How is God raising up others to join you in this vision? Through whom might He want to broaden the vision? Ask God to help you guard against defensiveness or pride. With humility, give Him the opportunity to bring openness to your mind and heart. Ask God to show you the people He wants to involve.

Ask the Lord to help you begin with the end in mind—begin with people! Ask these questions: Who is it we are seeking to serve through this vision? Who will be served in the church? Who will be served in the community? Who will be served among the unchurched? How might we best include and involve these people? How can they give us input about this vision?

God, because I know that I need other people's input and feedback for this vision . . .

Who might need to be consulted or given a chance to give input?

How might their contributions extend, improve, or enhance the overall vision?

How can I incorporate others' contributions?

Begin to summarize your time of prayer with the following sentence completion:

Our vision will be improved, enhanced, or extended as we incorporate . . .

I can better incorporate others' contributions to our vision after spending time in God's Word.

2. Spend time in God's Word, asking the Spirit to confirm the ways in which He wants you to incorporate others' ideas into your vision. What new growth might need to take place in you in order to prepare you for this process of incorporation? Do you need to . . .

- be quick to listen and slow to speak (James 1:19)?
- become more teachable (Proverbs 7:2)?
- become less prone to anger (Ephesians 4:26, 27)?
- be more humble or gentle (Matthew 11:29)?
- be more forgiving (Ephesians 4:32)?
- be more accepting (Romans 15:7)?
- speak words that edify or build up (Ephesians 4:29)?

After meditating on God's Word and considering how He might want to change you, complete the following:

The scriptural truth that might be most needed to prepare my heart for incorporating others' contributions is . . .

I can better incorporate others' contributions to our vision after prioritizing the needs of God's people.

3. Spend time discussing the vision with other people. Get input and feedback about the vision and how it would affect those you are seeking to serve. Ask yourself and others these questions:

How will this vision affect other people? Other ministries?

Who in the church is this vision intended to serve? Who in the community? Who among the unchurched?

How will we best involve those we seek to serve?

Who else might I need to discuss this vision with? Who else might need to be consulted or allowed to give input?

What other support might we need to accomplish this vision?

You may want to record these responses in the Team Journal at the end of the chapter.

Some specific tips for sharing vision and incorporating others' vision:
1. Give your team plenty of time to reflect on and receive what you have shared. Set aside one entire meeting to serve them with vision. Share the vision with a heart of servanthood—a spirit of humility and grace. Guard against a spirit of pride that holds too tightly to every detail of the vision, or a spirit of self-reliance that seems to communicate, "I can do this with or without you."

2. You might begin your time of sharing by saying, *God has burdened my heart concerning* _____, *and I could greatly benefit from your feedback. After I share my heart, I will be asking you to seek the Lord concerning this vision.*

I would like to share with you my vision and my sense of how God seems to be leading. During this time, I would like to give you the opportunity to ask questions and gain clarification so that you will be better prepared to prayerfully seek the Lord. I am looking forward to hearing how God impresses you, and receiving input He gives through you. At a later date, we will come back together to share the insights God has given to each of you.

3. After you share your vision with the team and allow them to ask questions, give them direction for the next step in the process:

You might say, *Reflect on this vision, spend some time in prayer, and then share with me the insight that God has given you. Let's get back together on _____. At that time, it would be a blessing to hear about your refinements and contributions to the vision. I would love to hear what you sense from the Lord about how this vision might honor Him and how you might be a part of it.*

You may also want to be vulnerable about the kind of input that would be difficult for you to receive. You might say, *When we get back together, it would mean a lot to me to hear your impressions from the Lord concerning this vision. It would be difficult though for me to hear _____ (e.g. criticism or evaluations). I will look forward to our next time together as we discover and confirm together where God is leading.*

(To help give guidance to each team member's time with the Lord, you may want to distribute the structured worksheet in Personal Exercise #5—*Being Served With Vision*.)

4. As you get back together to hear others' feedback, create an environment in which each person's input is taken seriously and their ideas are treated with honor and respect. Even if someone's ideas or perspectives are different from your own, communicate a desire to hear and understand. You may discuss possible ways to incorporate ideas as you meet together, but you may also want to suggest hearing all input and then giving everyone a chance to pray about the possible implications. This time span may give the Lord a chance to bring openness to ideas that might initially be dismissed.

After experiencing such a lengthy process of discerning vision, you may be wondering, "Why would I want to spend so much time in this process of discovery? Why should I invest such a great deal of energy into making every vision into a relational vision?" Leaders who remain committed to the process of relational vision will be blessed and encouraged both by the process of discovery and the final result of accomplishing God's will.

BENEFITS OF RELATIONAL VISION
As a relational leader works with his or her team to develop their relational vision, a multitude of benefits awaits the team and those they serve:

Relational Vision Instills Hope.
As relational leaders cast a vision and incorporate others' ideas, there begins to emerge an attitude of excitement and an expectancy that God will do great things. It is this environment of corporate hope that stirs up faith and helps us to believe that God can accomplish the impossible and achieve the inconceivable by His strength. This environment of expectant hope and faith touches the human spirit and clarifies the divine purpose for living. It begins to reveal the answer to the question, "Why am I here on this earth?" The unbelievers of our world are then attracted in a similar way as they see God's people hope in things beyond what we can see or hear. Discovering and implementing a relational vision draws the unbeliever to the One who inspires hope through our testimony of what only He can do.

Relational Vision Brings Security.
There is an increasing sense of certainty and direction as vision is defined, because without vision we are prone to wander around without purpose or focus (Proverbs 29:18). We gain a sense of security and purpose from knowing where we are going, and our hearts are filled with excitement and joy from knowing why we want to go there—to bring Him glory! In order to achieve this sense of security, each individual must examine the clarity of their life vision and maintain a focus on divine things instead of temporal ones. Unless our vision is centered on eternal things—God, His Word, and people— it will be impossible for us to keep God's priorities our priorities.

Relational Vision Builds Ownership.
People rarely reject ideas when they have contributed to them. Just as the human body is made up of many parts that are divinely designed to function with one another, so also is the church

(1 Corinthians 12:12–27). God's 21st century church is desperately in need of equipped saints for the work of the ministry (Ephesians 4:11, 12), and part of equipping this vast army of saints is allowing them to take ownership of a part of the vision for bringing others to Christ.

Relational Vision Stimulates Discipline.

Few of us can maintain discipline for its own sake. We need vision to keep us stimulated to maintain our Christian walk. Just as many of us fail to eat properly or exercise consistently without a definite goal for physical health, so it is with the spiritual disciplines. Fervent prayer and passionate worship lose their impact without the anticipation of divine vision. Joyful giving and committed fasting lose their urgency without a vision for things eternal. Committed passion for any of the Christian disciplines flows out of an experience with Jesus at the point of our need. It is the freshness of an ever-deepening walk with Jesus and commitment to the vision that He has birthed that keeps the relational leader's heart filled with gratitude and committed to the pursuit of Christlikeness.

Each of us must consider the significance of cultivating a deepened intimacy with Jesus through our times of prayer. It was the custom of Jesus and also part of the devotion of the apostles to spend time in meaningful prayer. Since prayerful discernment is a critical aspect of the vision process, each of us could probably benefit from experiencing the fulfillment of the disciples' cry: "Lord, teach us to pray" (Luke 11:1). After all, vision will only be entrusted to us and empowered within us as we maintain a depth of intimacy in our prayers to the One who originated it.

Consider the disciples' experience of often finding Christ in prayer. Imagine their unspoken question: "I wonder what He is praying about? Who is He praying for?" In the eleventh chapter of Luke, the disciples ask the Lord to teach them to pray. We do not even know which of the disciples asked the question, but we do know that much earlier (in Luke 6) the disciples were confronted with this startling reality: He has been praying for me! We can be certain of this reality because the Scriptures tell us that Christ had been praying all night on the mountain and, upon returning to the disciples, called them **by name** to come and be with Him so that He might send them out (Luke 6:12, 13; Mark 3:13–15).

Put yourself in the crowd that day as Christ returns from the mountain. He begins to call out certain names; one by one, Jesus addresses specific people. Suddenly, you hear Him call your name! Apparently, He has been praying for you!

Experiencing the Word Together

Consider the wonder of this personal truth:

"He always lives to make intercession for [you]" (Hebrews 7:25 NASB).

Imagine that you walk into a room and find Jesus in prayer. Picture Him praying, perhaps on bended knee or with His head bowed in humility. You may not hear the specific words, but you are confident that Christ is praying for someone He loves. You look over His shoulder and see your own prayer list lying in front of Him. He is praying for you, for your burdens, your temptations, and your heartfelt struggles. Imagine that He is praying for the very vision that you are being challenged to pursue.

How does it make you feel to know that Jesus prays for you? He intercedes on your behalf. He spends time talking to His Father about you—not judging or condemning, not in criticism or ridicule. Jesus speaks to the Father and reminds Him of your needs, reminds Him of the price He paid on the cross so that you might have abundant life both now and forever. How does it make you feel to reflect on Christ's prayers for you?

As I reflect on Christ's prayers for me, I am filled with . . .

Finally, consider the reality that He often prays for your needs and burdens without you! He prays alone. Is there something in your heart and spirit that prompts you to join Him more often? Is there a part of you that grieves when you imagine Christ praying alone?

Jesus, as I imagine You interceding for me—often without me—I feel . . .

I want You to hear the feelings of my heart concerning . . .

Finally, I am so grateful for Your . . .

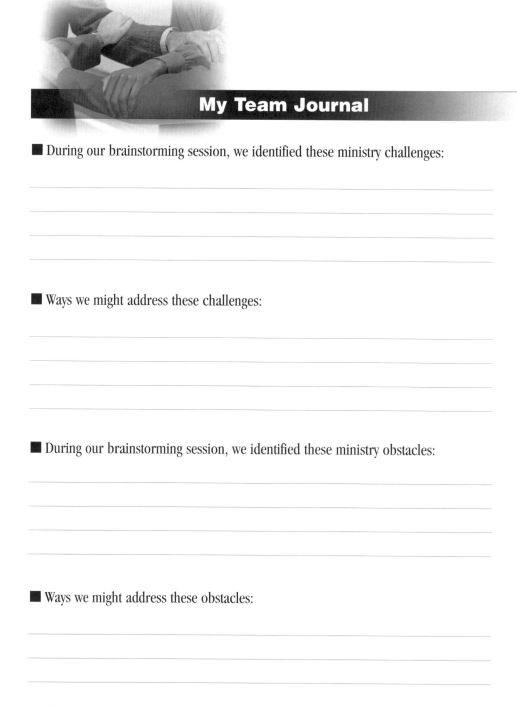

My Team Journal

◼ During our brainstorming session, we identified these ministry challenges:

◼ Ways we might address these challenges:

◼ During our brainstorming session, we identified these ministry obstacles:

◼ Ways we might address these obstacles:

■ We concluded that our team's vision relates to Christ's Great Commission in these ways:

_____

_____

_____

_____

■ How did each person summarize their sense of vision? Where do they sense God might be leading and why?

Name: Responses:

_____

_____

_____

■ What contributions to the vision did each person offer?

Name: Responses:

_____

_____

_____

■ What suggestions did the members have about incorporating others' contributions? Who should be consulted and how might their contributions improve the vision?

_____

_____

_____

_____

Chapter 6 Outline

I. **The Fundamentals of Discerning Vision: Three God-Centered Questions**
   A. Where Is God Leading?
      1. Our goal must be to discern what God wants to do, not just what **we** want to do.

      Personal Exercise #1

      2. We must resist the pull of man-centered vision originating from earthly concerns.
   B. Why Would God Lead Us There?
      1. We must seek to understand God's ways, His heart, His motivations.
      2. God made known His **deeds** to Israel, but He revealed His **ways** to Moses (Psalm 103:7).

      Personal Exercise #2

   C. Does Our Vision Reflect Concern for Eternal Things?
      1. Does our vision bring glory and honor to the Eternal One?

      Personal Exercise # 3

      2. Does our vision align with the eternal Word of God?

      Personal Exercise # 4

      3. Does our vision positively impact people, who are eternal?

II. **Moving From Individual Vision to Relational Vision**
   A. Typical Vision-Development Process
      1. "I have all the vision."
      2. "Someone else has all the vision."

B. Relational Vision-Development Process
   1. You are served with vision.

   Personal Exercise #5

   2. You courageously and creatively contribute to the vision.

   Personal Exercise #6

   3. You respectfully and resourcefully incorporate others' vision.

   Personal Exercise #7

III. **Benefits of Relational Vision**
   A. Relational Vision Instills Hope.
      1. That God will do great things
      2. That we are fulfilling our purpose for living
   B. Relational Vision Brings Security.
      1. We are going where God wants us to go.
      2. We are pursuing His goals, not our own.
   C. Relational Vision Builds Ownership.
      1. People rarely reject ideas when they have contributed to them.
      2. The body of Christ functioning—each part needing the others
         (1 Corinthians 12:21–27)
   D. Relational Vision Stimulates Discipline.
      1. Few people can maintain discipline for its own sake.
      2. Discipline that is sustained comes from clarity of vision concerning where we
         are going and why.

   Experiencing the Word Together

   My Team Journal

Additional Resources

George Barna, *The Power of Vision* (Ventura, CA: Regal Books, 2003).

Jim Herrington, R. Robert Creech, and Trisha Taylor, *The Leader's Journey: Accepting the Call to Personal and Congregational Transformation* (San Francisco: Jossey-Bass, 2003).

John C. Maxwell, *The Right to Lead* (Norcross, GA: Maxwell Motivation, Inc., 2001).

Dennis N. T. Perkins, et al., *Leading at the Edge* (New York: AMACOM, 2000).

John J. Westermann, *The Leadership Continuum* (Deer Lodge, TN: Lighthouse Publishing, 1997).

Chapter 7

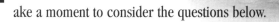

Implementing Relational Vision: Addressing Divine Objectives

T ake a moment to consider the questions below.

- What are Christ's priorities for your church or ministry?
- How would He evaluate the ministry that your church or team is currently carrying out?

Allow your reflections on Christ's priorities to give focus and direction as you complete this chapter.

Experts in church growth present various opinions about what makes a successful church. Some teach that churches must be seeker-friendly, or at least seeker-sensitive. Others argue that the key ingredients are a clear vision and a clear purpose, along with sound biblical doctrine. On most consultants' lists are an emphasis on outreach and missions, a comprehensive Bible study program, a strong worship ministry, and an effective organizational structure. While these ingredients may reflect valid needs, the most important question remains, "What matters most to Jesus?"

In the last chapter, we described a process for discerning vision relationally, and emphasized the fact that vision must be birthed from a concern for eternal things—God, His Word, and people. In this chapter, we will shift our focus to the implementation phase of relational vision. We will explore three divine objectives— unity, love, and witness—that should serve as guiding forces as you carry out the particular vision that you feel the Lord has ordained.

> **As relational leaders seek to implement vision, they must focus on the divine objectives of unity, love, and witness.**

These objectives are close to the heart of God, and pursuing them will allow you to carry out ministry that is truly successful in His eyes.

RELATIONAL LEADERS STRIVE TO PROMOTE UNITY.

"[I pray] that they may be one as we are one . . . May they be brought to complete unity to let the world know that you sent me and have loved them" (John 17:22, 23).

A few hours before He went to the cross, Jesus prayed to the Father for us, for those who would believe in Him (v. 20). Jesus' prayer revealed an issue of great significance. He asked for one thing with great clarity and boldness. He did not ask for us to be given great strength, or courage, or unshakable faith. Instead, Jesus prayed that we would experience oneness in our relationships. He asked that all those who believe in Him would achieve unity with each other as a visible reflection of divine unity. This plea for unity was more than a request that we share fundamental beliefs, visions, purposes, strategies, or programs. Christ's prayer reflected His desire for us to experience a depth of oneness that stems from a sincere love for Him and for one another.

As relational leaders minister within their churches or lay ministries, they may challenge their team to become more seeker-sensitive, assist with a transition to contemporary worship, or help to develop more comprehensive church programs. But as these and other issues are addressed, we must also focus on the greater eternal objective of unity, because it gives testimony to the divine mystery of oneness within the Godhead and speaks to a watching world about the One who sent us. Relational leaders must challenge others to live out a testimony of divinely-inspired unity.

What will this testimony of unity look like? How will the world know that Christ has been sent to us and has sent us to declare His love to others?

Unity Means "We Are Parts of One Body."

"The body is a unit, though it is made up of many parts; and though all its parts are many, they form one body" (1 Corinthians 12:12).

The apostle Paul used the human body to illustrate the unity of Christ's church, arguing that just as the body is composed of many parts, the church is made up of a myriad of important components. Every believer has been spiritually grafted into the body of Christ. Some have become figurative "hands" by serving others in the church. Others have become "mouths" as they preach or teach the Word of God.

God is the one who designs and creates the body and ordains the role that each person plays. He arranges each part of the body as He wishes, bringing unity from a diversity of gifts, talents, and experiences. His call is irreversible: "And if the ear should say, 'Because I am not an eye, I do not belong to the body,' it would not for that reason cease to be part of the body" (v. 16). This attitude of "one body, many parts" leads to unity because it gives perspective to each individual member of the body. It carries with it an implied imperative: "I'm a unique, important part of a larger whole. Therefore, I must find my place of service in the body."

As relational leaders serve those whom God has called them to lead, it is critical that they see their own unique contributions to the vision or ministry within the context of the larger whole. Leaders need to maintain a perspective that allows them to say, "As the Spirit has connected us to Christ as the Head, we are in fact connected to one another!" Relational leaders see the unique vision God has for their own lives, and understand how these callings fit into the vision that God has for the church as a whole. Thus, they are able to be confident in their own contributions while humbly acknowledging the equal importance of others' roles.

After gaining a strong sense of their own place in the body of Christ, relational leaders are able to cultivate an atmosphere of unity by recognizing and affirming the unique call on each of their team members' lives. In this environment of mutual encouragement, team members feel a sense of worth because their personal contributions are valued, their vision incorporated, and their skills and gifts appreciated. As leaders model this message of "We are parts of one body," their team members gain a sense of belonging, and gratefully receive a fuller understanding of how they fit into the multifaceted body of Christ.

In addition to affirming the gifts and callings of others, relational leaders must also demonstrate care and concern at the most fundamental level. They should rejoice when one part of the body is lifted up rather than becoming jealous or feeling threatened, and should mourn when any part of the body suffers (Romans 12:15). Through this kind of caring responsiveness, relational leaders will clearly communicate that "You are the body of Christ, and each one of you is a part of it" (1 Corinthians 12:27). It is this principle of being parts of one body that allows for the mutual experience of rejoicing together and hurting together.

Unity is therefore produced as each believer seeks to fulfill the role in the body that God has chosen for him or her. In a culture characterized by alienation and disconnectedness, the body of Christ, functioning in unity, has much to offer. In the midst of rampant loneliness, the church must be able to offer true fellowship that affirms each person's worth, provides each person with a sense of belonging, and confirms each person's calling for Kingdom life. Without such unity, the church is "of the world" as well as "in the world" (John 17:15, 16).

Personal Exercise #1

Reflect on your own contributions to the body of Christ. As you gain insight from the Lord concerning your place in the body, complete the following sentences:

God seems to have given me the spiritual gift(s) of _____ as a part of my role in the body.

God has blessed me with certain talents and skills in order to serve the body of Christ. Those skills and talents include . . .

God has led me through certain life experiences that I can bring to the body of Christ. Those experiences include . . .

My Team Journal #1

Share your responses to Personal Exercise #1 with your small group. Record each person's reflections on their own unique place in the body of Christ.

Name	Spiritual Gifts	Talents/Skills	Life Experiences
_____	_____	_____	_____
_____	_____	_____	_____
_____	_____	_____	_____
_____	_____	_____	_____
_____	_____	_____	_____

As you share, be open for others in your team to offer their impressions and affirmations about your gifts, talents, skills, and life experiences. Be sure to help confirm how God has blessed each member of the group.

Unity Means "We Need Each Other."

The apostle Paul elaborated on a second attitude that produces unity when he focused on the necessity of interdependence within Christ's church: "The eye cannot say to the hand, 'I don't need you!' . . . On the contrary, those parts of the body that seem to be weaker are indispensable" (1 Corinthians 12:21, 22). Paul argued that each member of the body needs the others. Members of the body of Christ are mutually dependent as they exercise their distinct gifts and callings.

Relational leaders must cultivate an atmosphere of interdependence by . . .

- offering consistent testimony of their need for both God and others.
- pursuing a relational vision to which many others may contribute their insights and leadings from the Lord.
- vulnerably sharing how others in the body have blessed, served, and ministered to them personally.
- deferring to others and, at times, submitting to others in recognition of the ways in which God has gifted other parts of the body (Ephesians 5:21).

Relational leaders must be comfortable needing others and frequently giving testimony to that fact. In turn, they will lead people toward an appreciation for how God has involved others in their lives and foster recognition of this mutuality of need.

Leaders who have a strong sense of interdependence ask of others and themselves, "Where would we be if someone had not shared the gospel with us? Where would we be if it were not for the teachers and mentors who invested in us?" Relational leaders acknowledge that we cannot fulfill our own ministry without being mutually dependent upon others. An attitude of interdependence produces an atmosphere in which believers look to meet the needs of others in the body. As these needs are met, the church moves forward in unity.

The 1st century church was guided by this objective of unity, and it was their desire to promote oneness within the body of Christ that gave rise to their actions and strategies. At one point, certain widows were being overlooked in the daily distribution of food. The disciples, recognizing the importance of their ministry of the Word and prayer, appointed deacons to serve and wait tables. Scripture then tells us that "This proposal pleased the whole group (they **united** around it) . . . so the word of God spread" (Acts 6:5, 7). This spirit of cooperation was in sharp contrast to the alienating and fragmented 1st century world. Similarly, when today's church functions in unity, expressing attitudes of humility and mutual support, it has much to offer an unbelieving world.

Personal Exercise #2

Reflect on your own experience of interdependence. Then complete the following sentences:

I recall a time when I needed _____(tell the person's name) *and their* _____ (*gifts, talents, expertise, advice, counsel, comfort, wisdom,* or *life experience*).

The Lord used their (*gift, talent, expertise,* etc.) *in my life to bring* _____ _____ (*encouragement, comfort, affirmation,* etc.).

Share your responses with your small group or partner as directed by your facilitator.

Unity Means "We Care About Each Other."

In two short verses, the apostle Paul presents another powerful characteristic of unity: an attitude of mutual concern. "So that there should be no division in the body, but that its parts should have equal concern for each other. If one part suffers, every part suffers with it" (1 Corinthians 12:25, 26). To be concerned about others is to express the very heart of God. God's concern is revealed in the Book of Acts, which speaks of His care for the Gentiles (Acts 15:14). His loving care is further illustrated in the Book of Jonah, which closes with a rhetorical question from God to Jonah: "Should I not be concerned about that great city?" (Jonah 4:11). These passages confirm God's character: it would be contrary to His very nature not to be concerned. And so it should be for those who have become partakers of His divine nature (2 Peter 1:4 KJV).

The apostle Paul also affirmed the link between mutual concern and unity through his own experience with the Corinthian church. The Corinthians expressed concern for Paul at difficult times in his ministry and made a significant impact on the apostle. Paul spoke of the Corinthians' "deep sorrow" and "ardent concern" on his behalf, with the result that "My joy was greater than ever" (2 Corinthians 7:7). It was clear, however, that the feeling of concern was mutual as Paul wrote, "I face daily the pressure of my concern for all the churches. Who is weak, and I do not feel weak? Who is led into sin, and I do not inwardly burn" (11:28, 29)? Mutual concern was experienced and unity was the result. The relationship between Paul and the church at Corinth was a great example of God's people caring for one another.

Relational leaders live out this same concern for others, expressing care and showing support. Effective leaders understand that our need for one another is mutual and that unity is produced as we give and receive care. Just as the church at Corinth showed ardent concern for Paul, so we must bear one another's burdens and fulfill the law of Christ (Galatians 6:2). In a world where love seems to have grown cold (Matthew 24:12), expressions of loving care within the body of Christ allow the world to know that we are His disciples (John 13:35).

Personal Exercise #3

Pause now and reflect on your own experience of care and concern within your team. Consider a time when something positive happened and a team member rejoiced with you. Or you might remember a time when something painful was going on in your life and a member of your team hurt with you and comforted you. Perhaps you were lonely and someone took thought of you. Maybe you were discouraged and someone encouraged you.

Complete the following sentence:

I remember being cared for by one of my team members when . . .

Share your responses with your small group or partner as directed by your facilitator.

Experiencing the Word Together #1

"Make every effort to keep the unity of the Spirit through the bond of peace" (Ephesians 4:3).

Consider an area of your ministry in which unity is needed. In what area might your team benefit from an additional sense of oneness?

We could benefit from a testimony of additional unity in . . .

Using the early church as your example (Acts 2:42–47; 6:1–7), what direction, insight, or guidance might you apply in your pursuit of unity in this area?

In order to have an increased sense of unity in this area of ministry, it might be important for us to consider . . .

(You may want to use the Relational Vision-Development Process from Chapter 6 to brainstorm ideas.)

RELATIONAL LEADERS EMPHASIZE THE IMPORTANCE OF LOVE.

"A new command I give you: Love one another. As I have loved you, so you must love one another. By this all men will know that you are my disciples" (John 13:34, 35).

In the previous chapter, you no doubt identified important areas of vision from the Lord. You and your team may now be in the midst of planning and implementing the details of that vision. Your leadership may certainly address the expansion of church activities, the recruitment and training of leaders, or the promotion of Christ's cause in the community, but relational leaders who approach these issues within the context of true fellowship will emphasize a more foundational, eternal objective: establishing God's church as a people of love.

As the above passage from John makes clear, the world will only know we are Christ's disciples if our lives are marked by His love. Tragically, an examination of 21st century Western society suggests that this identity of love has largely been lost, with serious consequences for both secular culture and the church.

The Decline of Love in Western Culture

Secular factors. Numerous factors have contributed to the steady decline of expressed love within our culture. The 20th century began with the rise of rationalism and secularism and culminated with a collection of notable but misdirected scholars asserting that "God is dead." Accompanying this was a progressive intolerance for spiritual and religious freedom in public life. Rising theological liberalism has, for many, undermined confidence in God, His Word, and His activity in the affairs of men. A pluralistic religious society in which many versions of "truth" are viewed as being equal has hastened the undermining of Judeo-Christian values.

This gradual deterioration of belief has in turn birthed many other forms of moral and societal decay. Decades of mobility, fragmented families, individual isolation, and countless other factors have weakened our ability to love. Serious dysfunction in a vast portion of the population (including substance abuse and other addictions, violence, sexual abuse, abandonment, and divorce) has rendered a significant part of three generations "functionally inadequate" when it comes to love. Extended families are often not available for parents to draw support from as they learn how to love their children. Marriages that were once supported, instructed, and encouraged by extended family members, institutions, and society are now left to fend for themselves. School systems are certainly not able to teach our children to love, since educators frequently find themselves teaching classes on tolerance, anti-violence, and conflict resolution. Even churches, which once provided social learning experiences and opportunities for close families, now often schedule activities that isolate individuals and separate families. Indeed, though it may seem shocking at first, we must realize that the church itself has contributed greatly to the lack of love in our contemporary culture.

Factors within the church. We have listed below some of the factors that have caused the church to become ineffective in equipping its members to demonstrate love. This inability to love has in turn rendered many of us ineffective as we have sought to reach an unbelieving world. Read this list carefully. Do any of these things apply to your team, church, or denomination?

Love grows cold when we . . .

- focus only upon people's sin and neglect to minister to their aloneness.
- label others' God-created relational needs "wrong" or view them as evidence of weakness, rather than encouraging vulnerable sharing and striving to meet the needs that others express.

- exalt self-reliance as if it is maturity, rather than equating maturity with humble interdependence.
- use "right beliefs" and "right behaviors" as substitutes for genuine Christlikeness.
- content ourselves with simply teaching and preaching biblical truth rather than truly giving of ourselves and sharing our lives with others.
- present the world with an evangelical message that self-righteously declares, "You need God," rather than proclaiming the whole truth: "We all need God and one another."
- emphasize an "us against them" philosophy rather than "us **for** them."

Personal Exercise #4

Review the list of hindrances to love within the church. Not only do these misconceptions and messages hinder the effective testimony of God's love, but over time they can develop into established ministry philosophies. Identify at least one of these things that might be hindering your love for others. Then identify at least one that might be hindering your ministry's love for others.

I sometimes tend to …

(For example: *I sometimes tend to operate with an attitude of self-reliance, communicating to others "I don't need you, and it's not OK for you to need me." I know that has resulted in several people describing me as "hard to get to know" or even "cold and indifferent.")*

We sometimes tend to …

(For example: *We sometimes tend to see only the sin in an individual's life and never even consider the loneliness that might be underneath the surface. I know there are some in our church who have felt condemned and have distanced themselves from active involvement within our congregation because of the judgment they perceived.)*

Share your conclusions and observations with your partner or small group.

The Motivation to Love: God's Love for Us

One particularly significant factor in the church's hindered display of love has been its myopic focus on rational truth. As teachers and pastors across the country have prepared, presented, and packaged biblical truth, they have almost exclusively addressed the rational mind rather than the relational heart of the hearer. Too many church leaders only teach, train, and equip the body of Christ with the cognitive truths of Scripture instead of leading them into a relational experience with the One who wrote the Word. The sustaining will to love and the ability to establish an environment of love can only come from an intimate walk with the God who **is** love (1 John 4:8). It is His love that motivates us toward selfless giving, unconditional sacrifice, and compassionate care.

In order to achieve this kind of intimacy with God, we must look beyond the rational truths of Scripture with which we are so familiar and examine the relational heart behind them. Consider, for example, the Ten Commandments. Typically, preachers and teachers emphasize the context in which they were given, the behavioral lifestyle they exhort, and the truthful insights they provide into God's character and holiness. But when we study the Ten Commandments and do not experience the heart of the compassionate Father who gave them to us, we cannot fully see the God who is love. Love grows cold when we see only the "Thou shalt not's" and miss out on the heart behind the commandments. A relational focus would lead us to ask the question, "Why did God give us these ten commandments?" Was it to raise a standard of moral behavior? Yes. Was it to give testimony of a righteous God? Of course. But at the same time, these commandments were given to us by a loving Father who did not and does not want to see His children hurt themselves or one another. Deuteronomy 10:13 speaks of these commandments being given "for your own good." What "good" does God have in mind for us? This focus on relational (rather than rational) truth enables us to see our caring Father and draws us into a more loving relationship with Him. This relational view of the Ten Commandments allows us to know the motive of love behind the standards and makes our heart receptive to a relationship with God.

Another important issue of which we often lack a relational understanding is God's response to our sinfulness. We often focus only on the darkness of our sin, thus failing to recognize the compassion of our loving Father, who is saddened that we have been hurt by our sin. There must be a balance between God's feelings toward sin and His feelings toward the sinner. Does God hate our immorality, selfishness, and pride? Absolutely. Yet at the same time, His heart is broken as He sees His children hurting because of their sin. God grieves for the husband who chooses an adulterous relationship, hurting for both the family members who are affected by the affair **and** the man who suffers the consequences of his behavior. God is saddened when He sees haughty pride in one of His daughters. He is opposed to her sin, yet brokenhearted because her self-reliance keeps her alone. It is this distinction between God's response to sin and His response to us as sinners that will prompt a greater love for the Father. Recognition and experience of this kind of love will empower the church to love others in the same way.

Experiencing the Word Together #2

"Give thanks to the Lord, for he is good" (Psalm 107:1).

Take the next few moments to refocus upon the relational truth that accompanies the rational truth with which you are familiar.

First, reflect on God's motive as He gave the Ten Commandments to Moses and the children of Israel. Why did He give them?

Yes, God gave the commandments in order to give testimony of His character, to portray righteous living, and to clarify sin's darkness. But we must look deeper into the Father's heart. He also gave the Ten Commandments because He knew how deeply our sin would hurt us. He gave them because He did not want to see us hurt. Like a loving parent would warn a child not to play in the street, God's heart of love and compassion motivated Him to establish rules and commandments because He knows that when we violate them, it hurts us. Consider again the "Thou shalt not's" of Scripture. How do you feel toward the Father as you reflect on this compassionate aspect of the Father's motive?

As I consider the loving motive behind God's gift of the Ten Commandments, I feel . . .

As I reflect on His heart for my good and His desire to protect me, I am filled with . . .

Share your responses with your partner or group as directed by your facilitator.

"The Lord longs to be gracious to you; he rises to show you compassion" (Isaiah 30:18).

Next, imagine the following scene: you watch from a distance as your young child chooses to violate a rule you have clearly set on the playground. You have given specific instructions not to go to the highest point of the jungle gym. You quickly leave your bench and approach the playground equipment, ready to remove your child. Before you can intervene, however, your child falls from the jungle gym and is hurt. The injury is minor, but your child is in pain.

In this situation, you would undoubtedly be filled with a mixture of emotions—righteous anger because she broke the rule, initial anxiety as you determined the extent of her injuries, all mixed with sadness because she was hurt. You would feel sorrow because of your child's pain even though the pain resulted from breaking a rule.

Our heavenly Father, who is both holy and loving, must have a similar reaction to us when we break the rules. Meditate on how His heart breaks when your sin hurts **you**. How does it make you feel to consider, perhaps for the first time, that God must be filled with a mixture of emotions when you sin? He hates the sin because He is holy, but at the same time, He is saddened by how your sin is hurtful to you. He experiences sorrow for your pain even when the pain results from breaking a rule.

Consider again the truth of Isaiah 30:18, and record your reflections as you think about how this new perspective could deepen His "constraining love" within you.

Heavenly Father, I am filled with _____ as I reflect on Your gracious and compassionate response to me and my sin.

I desire to be _____ toward others as I reflect on my gratefulness for Your love for me even in the midst of my sin.

Ways That Love Can Be Demonstrated

All ministry flows out of loving relationships, beginning with God and extending to others. The more that true intimacy and love is present within our relationships, the greater the potential for genuine and long-lasting ministry.

Now that you have discussed possible hindrances to loving others, and reflected on God's love for you, you will want to identify specific changes that need to occur. Spend time contemplating, "What improvements can be made to increase our ability to demonstrate love to an unbelieving world?" Below is a list of suggestions to consider.

A church or ministry that wishes to model the love of Christ will distinguish itself by . . .

- providing frequent and consistent opportunities to focus on and share gratefulness for abundant blessings received.
- challenging each member to develop a deepened understanding of a few people's key relational needs, beginning with their family members and close friends.
- facilitating frequent learning exercises and experiences where members are allowed to practice demonstrating love to one another.
- having its leaders model the giving of appreciation, attention, and comfort in each ministry setting so that members will see what love in action looks like and be able to give to others in return.
- encouraging members to consistently ask themselves "How am I giving to others?" and "How am I giving to God?" rather than "What am I getting out of church?"
- having its members gratefully and spontaneously minister to others, without the typical pleading and prompting from leaders.
- rejecting a focus on endless activity and competitive performance in favor of an emphasis on mutual caregiving and servanthood.
- making relationships and friendships for couples, families, and singles (rather than calendared events) the focus of its ministry.

A third eternal objective should guide our steps as we implement the vision God has given. The world will only come to know Him as we present an effective witness.

RELATIONAL LEADERS PRESENT AN EFFECTIVE WITNESS.
"And you will be my witnesses" (Acts 1:8).

With these few words, Christ empowered His church to take the Gospel message into all the world. How is the 21st century church doing at achieving this eternal goal? How well is the church of the Western world giving testimony about our relationship with Christ?

Recent surveys indicate that a majority of non-Christians consider spiritual things to be very important in their lives. Studies also show that many non-Christians look to God and the church for help in times of discouragement and trouble. It is encouraging to learn that unbelievers are looking for answers in the right places. But are they finding them?

Upon further study, we find that an overwhelming majority of non-Christians feel that the church is not sensitive to their real needs. They find our message is often irrelevant, that it is not clearly applicable and pertinent to their needs. Hurting people are looking for answers in the right place, but often leave frustrated because the church's solutions do not consistently meet their needs.

We know the Gospel message itself is certainly good news for hurting people. It proclaims that Christ died for our sins, was buried, and was raised on the third day (1 Corinthians 15:3, 4). The impasse between God and man was fully addressed by a gift, the only gift that would satisfy His righteousness. That gift was a perfect sacrifice without spot or blemish, the gift of Himself through His only begotten Son. Romans 5:8 reminds us that God demonstrated His love for us by sending Christ to die for us while we were sinners.

If a large percentage of non-Christians feel that the church's message is not clearly applicable, and this lack of relevance cannot be attributed to the Word of God, the problem must be with the messengers. We must conclude that the church is failing to effectively witness to the rest of the world about the gospel of Jesus Christ. Relational leaders must be able to lead their team in effectively proclaiming Christ with a sensitivity and relevance that our culture finds immediately pertinent to their needs. How can the church give effective witness to those needing a personal relationship with God?

Bearing Witness to a Need-Meeting God

"We are therefore Christ's ambassadors, as though God were making his appeal through us" (2 Corinthians 5:20).

As the church seeks to be more effective ambassadors of Christ, it must become more than just a defender and propagator of truth. In a relativistic world that lacks the framework of absolute truth, it is essential that we hold fast to the absolutes of God and His Word, but the church must become more than a place where people believe and proclaim the Truth. It must be a place where we take the initiative to establish relationships with a hurting world. It must be a place where we declare, "God is concerned with our needs! He is a need-meeting God!" We need His forgiveness, and He offers it. We need acceptance, comfort, and hope, and He longs to give them. He generously gave up His Son that our needs for forgiveness and for an intimate relationship with Him would be fully addressed. Just as God has acted to meet our needs, we must take specific steps to meet the needs of those who lack a relationship with Him if we hope to be effective witnesses for the cause of Christ.

In Philippians 4:19, Paul declares, "My God will meet all your needs." The context of the verse substantiates the fact that although God sometimes meets our needs directly, He often meets them through others. In verse 14, Paul says, "It was good of you to share in my troubles," and in verse 16 he states that "When I was in Thessalonica, you sent me aid again and again when I was in need." He emphasizes the fact that God involves members of His body to meet people's needs when he instructs the church at Rome to "Share with God's people who are in need" (Romans 12:13). In the same way, effective relational leaders will look for opportunities to meet the needs of those around them. In so doing, they will give testimony to an unbelieving world about the God who abundantly meets needs.

By unfortunate contrast, the church has often presented a skewed picture of God by sending the message that "God is only concerned about your 'fallenness.' He is only concerned about sin." God **is** concerned about our sin, but He is also concerned about our needs. The rare expression "My God" in Philippians 4:19 paints a picture of the apostle "bragging" on His God as One who meets needs. In a world of "sin inspection," we must become a people who boldly give witness to our need-meeting God. This good news should not only encourage our hearts, but should set the agenda for what and how we must share with others. As we share God's love with hurting people, we must communicate both His desire for righteousness and His longing to provide for their needs.

Relational leaders understand that this prioritizing of needs must affect our approach to evangelism. Instead of trying to convince people to believe what we believe, relational leaders realize that we must lovingly represent a God who cares for people and wants to meet their needs. It is because of His loving heart that God wants to meet our need for the forgiveness of sins, which makes a meaningful relationship with Him possible. As we make this transtion from a belief-based witness to a needs-based one, we must . . .

- move from a "come and see" focus to a "go and share" focus.
- take initiative to minister to those outside the church, as Jesus did.
- consider the reputation of Jesus as a "friend of sinners" (Matthew 11:19), and let it shape our witness to those around us.
- create an environment of mutual giving within the body of Christ as relational needs are made known and met.
- equip ourselves in the relational skills that will allow us to meet people's needs for acceptance, comfort, encouragement, approval, security, and respect—both within the body of Christ and among others.

Personal Exercise #5

I personally could benefit from . . .

- *becoming more "go and share" focused.*
- *taking more initiative to care for those outside the church.*
- *being less sin-focused and more of a friend to sinners.*
- *being more open to receive from others at the point of my need, and more sensitive and attentive to other's needs.*
- *becoming better equipped in the relational skills of meeting needs as I learn how to live out the "one anothers" of Scripture.*

As you reflect upon your team's vision and objectives, how could the five items above provide confirmation and direction?

Our team could benefit from prayerful consideration of _____
(choose one of the five items).

Share your responses with your team and then pray with a partner concerning these matters.

Bearing Witness to The Priority of Relationships

Relational leaders should not only give testimony of a God who meets needs, but of One who prioritizes relationships. Effective leaders know that drawing the contemporary unbeliever will require more than mandates on what to believe or how to behave. Doctrine, theology, and Bible knowledge are all important fields of cognitive study, but they are not sufficient to entice a skeptical world. Propositions and precepts are not to become our identity. Relational leaders must be able to communicate the heart of God, offering a deep, intimate friendship with Him.

The church of the 21st century will be challenged to focus upon the relational aspects of Christ's ministry if they hope to impact the world. Relational leaders must guide their team and impress on the hearts of other leaders the importance of ministering like Jesus. Our Savior lived as a "friend to sinners." He focused upon relationships and then allowed the Holy Spirit to bring repentance to lives.

The story of Zacchaeus the tax collector displays the impact that the powerful love of Christ can have on an individual. Jesus offered Zacchaeus a relationship filled with acceptance and affirmation. Only afterward did the Holy Spirit prompt a change in Zacchaeus' behavior (Luke 19). Christ also displayed His heart for relationships as He responded to the woman caught in adultery. There is often speculation about what Jesus wrote in the dirt as He knelt beside the woman who had been caught in the very act of sin. But more important than what Christ wrote is the reason **why** He knelt beside the woman. Jesus knelt beside this woman because she needed acceptance, security, and someone to help her face the angry conspirators. The Savior offered no condemnation, sermon, or accusation, and only after reassuring the woman of His own compassion did He say, "Go now and leave your life of sin" (John 8:1–11). There were other times when Jesus focused on relationships and did not even address someone's spiritual condition. Mark tells us that a man with leprosy came to Jesus and begged for healing. Christ healed the man without ever addressing spiritual issues (Mark 1:40–45). Christ's provision for the four thousand on the hills of Galilee is another example of His commitment to meet relational and physical needs apart from the spiritual. He was moved with compassion and abundantly met the needs of the crowd that day without mention of spiritual things (Matthew 15:32–39). Our Savior was able to simply demostrate compassionate care and then trust the Holy Spirit to draw people to Him.

Effective relational leaders will model their leadership after the ministry of Christ as they . . .

- cultivate caring relationships with those outside the church.
- trust God to convict others about their sin rather than considering it their job to point out the sin in the lives of others.
- focus less on propositional arguments for the faith in favor of presenting an incarnate witness as "living letters."
- remove judgment from their hearts as they graciously accept those who are away from Christ, realizing that they walk in darkness and need the light of our lives.

Relational leaders must also focus on fulfilling the Great Commandment by cultivating a deep personal love for God. As Christian leaders, we can often become so distracted by the busyness of ministry that we neglect knowing God personally and intimately. We can easily mistake pursuing ministry for pursuing a relationship with God. As leaders, we may read the Bible to prepare for the next sermon or lesson, but how often do we meditate on Scripture solely to know God's heart? We focus on the facts about God and the programs of the church, but how much time is spent hearing His heart? In order for relational leaders to be equipped to lead their team toward the vision God has for them, they must first have an intimate relationship with God that . . .

- gives witness to the humility of dependence: "I do nothing on my own initiative" (John 5:19, 20).
- gives witness to an expectant faith—anticipating and longing for God's revelation, provision, and empowerment.
- gives witness to the wonder of gratitude—being filled with the inexpressible joy of fresh encounters with Him.
- gives witness to our secure identity as His beloved—being free from defensiveness, being easily entreated and approachable.

Effective vision and witness must begin with your relationship with the Creator, through His Son, Jesus Christ. It is personal stories of this wonderful love and how it has impacted your life that will draw others to Him.

After addressing his or her own relationship with the Lord, the relational leader must also challenge the church to encourage loving relationships, beginning at home. The church of the 21st century must prioritize family relationships and provide the tools necessary to strengthen them. The concentric circles of ministry presented in the witnessing strategy of Acts 1:8 (Jerusalem, Judea and Samaria, the ends of the earth) must be applied not only to our evangelism but also to our witness of Great Commandment love, beginning with those nearest us. Relational leaders must . . .

- freely receive from the Lord's wonderful love, and then freely give to those in their "Jerusalem," those with whom they have the closest relationships—their spouses, children, family members, and close friends (Matthew 10:8).
- make their own marriages reflections of how much Christ loves His church (Ephesians 5:25). Leaders must be able to give this invitation: "If you would like to see God's forgiveness, acceptance, and grace in the lives of real people, then come to my home. Come talk with me and my spouse."
- make their own parenting a witness to the way that God cherishes each of His children as special gifts. Leaders must be able to give this invitation: "If you would like to see God's attentive care, sensitive compassion, and understanding heart, come spend time with our family."
- make their single adult friendships testimonies to the integrity and intimacy with which Christ (as a "single adult") loved His cherished friends—Mary, Martha, and Lazarus (John 11:1–44).

Church vision must provide for ongoing relational ministries for singles, couples, parents, and families—ministries that foster growing intimacy and equip individuals to meet relational needs. It is this sharing of love with God and others that challenges us to live out what we believe. Loving our "nearest ones" is what challenges our self-focus, brings accountability to our proclamations, and lends integrity to our witness. After all, the Christian life was always intended to be lived out first with a few people who are nearest to us. Then our focus should extend to a few others, including His church, and then to a watching world.

Personal Exercise #6

Consider the concentric circles of Great Commandment love and reflect on where a deepened work might be needed in you.

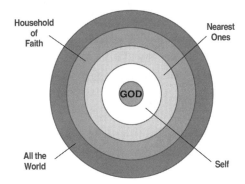

I need a deepened experience and expression of love . . .

- *toward God—embracing the wonder of His grace.*
- *toward myself—gaining security in my identity as His beloved.*
- *toward my spouse—making our marriage more of a witness to His enduring love.*
- *toward my children/family/friends—giving witness to a God who cherishes people as special gifts.*

Next, take a few moments and assess your church or ministry's focus and any changes that might need to be made.

Considering the concentric circles above, our ministry vision could benefit from an additional emphasis on. . . .

Share your responses with your team members or partner. Spend time in prayer, asking for God's direction and revelation as it relates to living out His Great Commandment love.

Bearing Witness by Sharing the Gospel and Our Lives

"We loved you so much that we were delighted to share with you not only the gospel of God but our lives as well" (1 Thessalonians 2:8).

The apostle Paul presented this powerful insight for communicating the Gospel as he wrote to the church of Thessalonica: share the written letter (the Gospel) and share the living letter (your life). This is a powerful combination. Paul iterated this dual emphasis in chapter one of 1 Thessalonians as well. "Because our gospel came to you not simply with words, but also with power, with the Holy Spirit and with deep conviction. You know how we lived among you for your sake" (1 Thessalonians 1:5). Relational leaders understand that in order to truly impact others with the Gospel, they must vulnerable share their own lives along with the truth of God's message.

There is a deep, costly commitment involved in sharing one's life with another person. It requires a supernatural and sacrificial love that draws others to Christ and bears much fruit. Relational leaders will therefore . . .

- insure that their walk matches their talk—that their "living letter" affirms the reality of the written Word.
- share vulnerly about their own Christian life, personal challenges, and relational needs, thus freeing others to "be real" as well.
- be moved more often with the compassion of Christ rather than resorting to impersonal exhortation and advice-giving.

Personal Exercise #7

Take a few moments to assess the environment of your own church or ministry:

How well do people in our church know one another?

Do they delve beyond doctrine, ministries, and events—beyond "believing right" and "behaving right" to deeper issues of the heart?

To what extent do they genuinely share their lives with one another—not just the good aspects of life, but also the sad, hurtful areas?

Does the vision for our church include a focus on team members sharing their lives with one another?

Does our vision include creative ways to share our lives with people outside the church?

Share your responses with your partner or small group as directed by your facilitator.

My Team Journal #2

As a summary and conclusion to this chapter, spend a few moments summarizing the needed changes you discussed with your team or partner.

■ As we reflected upon the eternal objective of unity within the body of Christ, we identified these areas of needed change:

_____

_____

_____

_____

■ As we reflected upon the eternal objective of love within the body of Christ, we identified these areas of needed change:

_____

_____

_____

_____

_____

■ As we reflected upon the eternal objective of becoming Christ's witnesses, we identified these areas of needed change:

_____

_____

_____

_____

_____

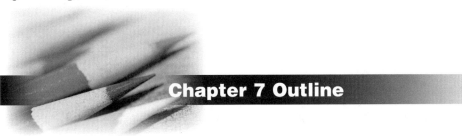

Chapter 7 Outline

I. Relational Leaders Strive to Promote Unity.
  A. Unity Means "We Are Parts of One Body" (1 Corinthians 12:12).
    1. Celebrate the specific gifts and contributions of others.
    2. Affirm each team member's divine calling.
    3. Demonstrate "equal care" by rejoicing with those who are honored and suffering with those who suffer (1 Corinthians 12:25, 26).

    Personal Exercise #1 and My Team Journal #1

  B. Unity Means "We Need Each Other" (1 Corinthians 12:21, 22).
    1. Developing vision relationally–insight of others is sought and incorporated.
    2. Vulnerably sharing how others have blessed, served, and ministered to us personally
    3. Submitting to others (Ephesians 5:21)

    Personal Exercise #2

  C. Unity Means "We Care About Each Other."
    1. The example of Paul and the Corinthian church (2 Corinthians 7:6, 7; 11:28, 29)
    2. Our need for care is mutual.

    Personal Exercise #3

    Experiencing the Word Together #1

II. Relational Leaders Emphasize the Importance of Love.
  A. The Decline of Love in Western Culture
    1. Secular factors
    2. Factors within the church

a. Focusing only upon people's sin and neglecting to minister to their aloneness
b. Labeling others' relational needs as "wrong" or viewing them as evidence of weakness
c. Exalting self-reliance as if it is maturity, rather than equating maturity with humble interdependence
d. Using "right beliefs" and "right behaviors" as substitutes for genuine Christlikeness
e. Being content with simply teaching and preaching biblical truth rather than truly giving of ourselves and sharing our lives with others
f. Presenting others with the message, "You need God," rather than "We all need God and one another."
g. Emphasizing an "us against them" philosophy rather than "us **for** them"

Personal Exercise #4

B. The Motivation to Love: God's Love for Us

Experiencing the Word Together #2

C. Ways That Love Can Be Demonstrated
1. Providing frequent opportunities to share gratefulness for God's abundant blessings
2. Challenging members to develop a deepened understanding of others' relational needs
3. Facilitating learning experiences where members are allowed to practice demonstrating love to one another
4. Having leaders model the giving of appreciation, attention, and comfort
5. Encouraging members to ask "How am I giving to others?" and "How am I giving to God?" rather than "What am I getting out of church?"
6. Having members spontaneously minister to others, without pleading and prompting from leaders
7. Rejecting a focus on endless activity and competitive performance in favor of an emphasis on mutual caregiving and servanthood
8. Making relationships and friendships (rather than calendared events) the focus of ministry

III. Relational Leaders Present an Effective Witness.
   A. Bearing Witness to a Need-Meeting God
     1. Move from a "come and see" witness to a "go and share" witness.
     2. Take initiative to minister to those "outside" the church.
     3. Become a "friend of sinners" (Matthew 11:19).
     4. Create an environment of safety.
     5. Equip others to meet the needs both of those within the body of Christ and those outside the church.

     Personal Exercise #5

   B. Bearing Witness to the Priority of Relationships
     1. Offer unbelievers more than mandates on what to believe or how to behave.
     2. Focus on relationships, allowing the Holy Spirit to motivate repentance where necessary.
     3. Emphasize the importance of personal love for God.
     4. Prioritize loving relationships with others, beginning at home.

     Personal Exercise #6

   C. Bearing Witness by Sharing the Gospel and Our Lives (1 Thessalonians 2:8).
     1. Insure that our walk matches our talk—that our "living letter" affirms the reality of the written Word. Invite others to give us honest feedback.
     2. Share vulnerably about our own Christian life, personal challenges, and relational needs, freeing others to "be real" as well.
     3. Be moved more often with the compassion of Christ, and rely less on exhortation, knowledge, or advice-giving.

     Personal Exercise #7

     My Team Journal #2

Additional Resources

John C. Maxwell, *Failing Forward* (Norcross, GA: Maxwell Motivation, Inc., 2000).

Fred Smith, "Secrets to Making Great Decisions," *Leadership Journal* vol. 16, no. 4 (1995): 92-97.

Helmut Thielicke, "Beyond Pushing and Producing," *Leadership Journal* vol. 16, no. 4 (1995): 84-87.

Chapter 8

Committing to the Pursuit of Growth

As we conclude our study of relational leadership, it is critical that we continue to pursue the kind of leadership that God desires for us. Even as you complete your work in this resource, we hope that you will continue to allow the Lord to complete the work that He has begun in you. The apostle Paul reminds us that as believers in Christ, we are being "fitted together" that we might grow into the likeness of Jesus (Ephesians 2:21, 22 NASB). As each of us is "fitted together" with our teams, our heavenly Father wants us to continue being conformed to the image of His Son. The relational leader exemplifies a life that is pleasing to the Lord as he or she consistently pursues growth. We must continue to submit ourselves to the transforming work of Christ, and commit to becoming growing people, who then grow other people, who, in turn, grow ministries.

> **Relational leaders must be committed to an ongoing process of personal, team, and ministry growth.**

Take a few moments to consider the questions below:

- As you complete this course of study, what plans do you have to implement the principles discussed in this resource?

- What are your plans for continued growth in your relationship with Christ? In your relationships with your spouse, children, or family? In your relationship with your ministry team?

- What hindrances to personal growth do you anticipate? What hindrances to your growth with your spouse, children, family, or team do you anticipate?

Now that you have considered how you will apply the principles of relational leadership and how you might continue your own personal growth, allow these reflections to give focus to this final chapter of relational principles.

CHARACTERISTICS OF MEANINGFUL GROWTH

Let us begin with an overview of the defining characteristics of meaningful growth. Personal, team, and ministry growth all depend upon these principles.

Meaningful Growth Will Be Sacrificial.

As you have experienced this course, you have undoubtedly observed an emphasis upon the necessity of servanthood. Inevitably, we will have to make sacrifices in order to fulfill the vision to which God has called us. Sacrifice is an unavoidable, undeniable element of servanthood. We know that the ministry of Jesus was characterized by the challenge to sacrifice. His disciples "left everything and followed Him," and were encouraged to count the cost before building their lives upon Him and even to lose their lives for His sake (Luke 5:11; 14:28–33, Matthew 10:39).

Sacrificial growth will occur as we encounter God at the point of His Word. As we present ourselves to the Lord as holy sacrifices, humbly acknowledging our need for His work in our lives and the convicting work of the Holy Spirit through the Word of Truth, we will begin to mature in the image of Christ. The cost of personal maturity and Christlikeness will be the relinquishment of our own selfish agendas, prideful preferences, and self-condemning messages in exchange for humble submission to the Word of God. Therefore, before we can begin to effectively lead the people whom God is calling us to serve, we must devote ourselves to fully experiencing His Word. There will be specific sacrifices that God will call us to make in order that we might grow personally, challenge others to grow, and lead them in growing a ministry.

What are some of the truths we must experience as relational leaders? How are we to become living sacrifices who present ourselves to God for spiritual service (Romans 12:1, 2 NASB)?

Personal Exercise #1

Reflect on the following biblical truths. Consider the extent to which you have experienced them in your life. Scripture tells us that God's Word is like a sharp, double-edged sword that judges the thoughts and attitudes of our hearts (Hebrews 4:12). Take a moment and ask the Lord to show you any attitudes, actions, or thoughts that need to be changed in you. Ask the Holy Spirit to bring conviction regarding any areas of needed growth.

Your prayer might sound like this:

Lord, what biblical truths do I need to further experience as I seek to live out the vision You have given our team? What sacrifices do I need to make in order to experience growth and become more like Christ? Please show me areas in which I need to grow.

- Do I need to "put away" my anger and become more tender-hearted and compassionate (Ephesians 4:31 NASB)?
- Do I need to learn to speak the truth in love, becoming more bold about speaking the truth or more loving in the way I convey the message (v. 15)?
- Do I need to speak words that "build up" rather than words that are critical, harsh, or inappropriate (v. 29)?
- Do I need to give honor or respect to others more frequently, being considerate with my tone of voice, asking rather than demanding, being careful to be on time, refraining from threats or condemnation, and valuing others' input and ideas (Romans 12:10)?
- Do I need to enter others' worlds more often by showing appropriate attentiveness and care (1 Corinthians 12:25)?
- Do I need to give more praise to others, offering words of appreciation for effort and accomplishment (Colossians 3:15; 1 Corinthians 11:2)?
- Do I need to show more acceptance of others' differences and uniqueness (Romans 15:7)?
- Do I need to demonstrate more comfort to others when they are hurting, giving a caring response to their pain rather than advice, comparison, or spiritual pep talks (12:15)?

- Do I need to demonstrate more affection with those closest to me, giving priority to communicating my care and heartfelt love (16:16; Mark 10:16)?
- Do I need to become more dependable, keeping my commitments, completing my responsibilities, and giving security to those around me (Romans 12:16–18)?
- Do I need to take more personal responsibility, having self-control over my behaviors, attitudes, and emotions? Do I regularly give an account of myself to God (14:12)?
- Do I need to increase my commitment to personal integrity, being careful to maintain personal convictions and let my "walk" be the same as my "talk" (Psalm 78:72)?

I believe that God might be at work in me, to change me in the area of . . .

These areas of needed growth will be discussed with your partner or small group during later exercises.

Meaningful Growth Will Be Mutual.

If we are to find the empowerment that God wants us to have for the vision He has put on our hearts, there must be a mutual commitment from God's people to encourage one another toward love and good deeds (Hebrews 10:24). Whether we are considering personal growth, growth among team members, or the growth of a ministry, the overwhelming message must be "We need each other in order to grow." Or, to phrase it another way, "We cannot grow ourselves **by** ourselves."

Relational leaders understand that we need one another in each of these areas of growth. Personal growth can only be accomplished within the context of the encouragement of the saints. Iron must sharpen iron. Truth must be shared in love. Feedback must be welcomed and input freely received.

Growth must also become a mutual effort as we build our team. When team members are able to openly share and tenderly care for one another, they create an atmosphere that provides the maximum opportunity for mutual growth. A leader who is vulnerable with his or her areas of needed growth challenges other team members to grow. An effective relational leader creates an environment where it is safe to be real about needed growth. As a climate of mutual respect and love is created, God is free to engage team members in mutual care and encouragement for one another.

Finally, the expansion and success of our ministry as a whole depends upon the extent to which **we** are committed to that growth. When a church seeks to expand its ministry through an evangelistic emphasis, conversion growth will only be achieved to the extent that both clergy and laity are committed to the goal. Growth of a ministry is only possible when the leaders and team members of that ministry are committed to discerning and fulfilling the vision God has for them. Ministries do not grow solely because of leaders who grow, but because of leaders who foster a sense of ownership, mutuality, and sacrifice among all the team. Growth of the ministry occurs when we are committed to the vision God has given "us," as opposed to the vision God has given "them."

Experiencing the Word Together

"This is the confidence we have in approaching God: that if we ask anything according to his will, he hears us. And if we know that he hears us—whatever we ask—we know that we have what we asked of him" (1 John 5:14, 15).

Spend a few moments reflecting again upon your responses to Personal Exercise #1. Allow the Holy Spirit to touch your heart with one or more of the ways you may need to grow. In which areas have you needed to experience more of His Word in your life? Realizing that you need others as you pursue personal growth, ask the Lord to bring people across your path that will challenge and encourage your growth.

Your prayer might sound like this:

God, as You see things about my life that are distracting to my presentation of Christ, I want to be open to You and to others that You may want to involve in bringing me back to the truth of Your Word. Could You please send someone into my life to point out these areas of needed growth? Please use those nearest to me—my family, my spouse, and my ministry team—to help me grow. Thank You for changing me.

Lord, I realize that I may need particular growth in the area of . . .

As a means of practicing the mutuality of growth, pray this prayer with a partner or your small group as directed by your facilitator.

Meaningful Growth Will Be Empowered by Gratitude.

Gratitude for what God has done is the empowering motivator for the relational leader. Significant personal growth is accomplished as a leader begins to reflect upon all that God has provided, all the "good and perfect" gifts that have come down from the Father in heaven (James 1:17). Christ must have often expressed His gratitude in prayer to the Father. The tenth chapter of Luke records a specific time when we sense the Savior's grateful heart upon the return of His disciples from a time of ministry. "At that time Jesus, full of joy through the

Holy Spirit, said, 'I praise you, Father, Lord of heaven and earth, because you have hidden these things from the wise and learned, and revealed them to little children'" (Luke 10:21). It is this same gratefulness for the ways in which the Lord has intervened on our behalf that motivates change and personal growth in the life of the leader. It is this thankfulness that prompts and sustains a changed life. It is gratitude that says to the Lord, "Based upon all You have done for me, I want to be more like You."

As relational leaders, we must first focus upon growth in our own lives. Only then are we ready to look toward the areas of needed growth in others. Here again, gratitude must empower and pervade our efforts. Team members will resist any leader whose motives are clearly selfish or prideful, but will be open to growth as they sense their leader's grateful heart. Team members will resist an approach that suggests, "I want you to change in this area because I'm tired of . . ." or "I want you to grow in this area because I would like to. . . ." Instead, a relational leader must be able to communicate a message of grateful motivation—"Christ has so blessed me that I don't want you to miss out on any blessing He has for you." Team members will be more open to personal change and more willing to take on responsibility in the vision as they sense their leader is creating an opportunity for their good.

When relational leaders pursue their commitment to grow themselves and, with a heart of gratitude, challenge others to grow as well, they will then have a team that is equipped to grow a ministry. Leaders who attempt to expand or grow a ministry with any motive other than a heart of gratitude will often face doubts from their team members, and questions about their motives. In such situations, team members are often hesitant to follow, and grow weary of merely fulfilling inescapable obligations.

As leaders attempt to fulfill the vision they believe God has ordained, they must not be motivated merely by a sense of duty or selfish ambition. As a team works toward fulfilling the vision God has for them, the members must sense that the only guiding motive is a pure heart of gratitude for how the Lord has demonstrated His loving care. Whether a team's vision relates to evangelism or more internal growth, gratitude must prevail. Evangelism is not to be a guilt-ridden response to men's pleadings, but rather a joyful imparting of the Gospel and one's very life (1 Thessalonians 2:7, 8). Ministry to others must not be a programmed attempt to fulfill one's religious duty, but rather a grateful display of sharing and caring that is motivated by the wonder of being loved by Him. A ministry's growth occurs as a team experiences such a degree of gratefulness for how God has blessed them and their ministry that they are compelled to pass along that blessing to others. It is this testimony of gratitude that reminds others that the vision, the ministry, the purpose is "all about Him"!

Now that we have discussed the priorities that should accompany all growth, we will turn our attention to three different dimensions of growth: personal growth, growing others, and growing a ministry.

RELATIONAL LEADERS DEMONSTRATE COMMITMENT TO PERSONAL GROWTH.

You have undoubtedly undergone a great transformation through your own journey with the Lord and we hope that your personal growth has continued as you have completed this course of study. We have encouraged you to grow in the areas of humility, faith, gratitude, and servanthood. We have given you the chance to grow in your relationship with Christ and with those He has called you to serve. Now we hope to encourage your personal growth as you become additionally equipped for transition through the various roles of ministry leadership. For the relational leader, personal growth involves learning to negotiate the transitions of ministry.

One of the most challenging times in any ministry is when God leads us through a transition. These transitions may occur as a church or ministry grows, as opportunities for new ministries increase, or as God moves and expands existing ministries. As you and your team seek to fulfill the vision God has given, you will inevitably face many of the "growing pains" that come with ministry expansion or development. Failure to recognize and successfully navigate these transitions may cause churches to stagnate and ministries to plateau. Research often identifies "attendance barriers" or "attendance ceilings" as indicators of a church or ministry's lack of growth. While many factors may contribute to these barriers or ceilings, relational leaders are prepared to face these challenges by first

> **One important aspect of personal growth is successfully navigating the transitions of ministry.**

addressing their own transitional roles. Throughout this portion of our text, we will discover how the leadership of Moses gives us insight into negotiating the transitions of ministry. These same leadership roles are also seen in the life of Christ, and you will no doubt recognize these principles as we explore them together.

Transitions of Ministry: "Being With" Your Team

In previous chapters, we have identified the starting place for creating a caring and connected team and recognized the relational leader's first role in ministry as "being with" your team. We have discussed the fact that before we lead others toward a vision or enlist their help with a particular goal, we must first come to know them and allow them to know us. Christ led by "being with" His disciples. He did not distance Himself from their lives and struggles, but lovingly invested in them.

Moses also exemplified this role of "being with" in his relationship with the children of Israel. Moses bore witness to God's power and wrath by calling down the ten plagues upon Pharaoh, but he also lived among the people as they witnessed these horrible afflictions and dealt with Pharaoh's continual refusals to let them go. It was through Moses' presence and commitment to "be with" them that the children of Israel came to know and trust their leader.

The relational leader's first role in ministry and initial step of growth is to "be with" his or her team. Only by getting to know your team (and allowing them to know you) will you enable them to trust you and to see your commitment to lead according to God's plan. You will have taken a first step in personal growth as you prioritize "being with" your people. They will be able to rest assured of your care, feel secure in your leadership, and be inspired by your servant's heart. Your investment in "being with" them will inspire humility, faith, and gratitude in their lives and will prepare them to serve the Lord in new ways as He leads you through other transitions.

Personal Exercise #2

Take the next few moments and reflect on your time spent with your partner or team during this course. You may also want to reflect on time spent with other ministry teams. Consider the blessings that have come from "being with" others. How have you and your team benefited from your commitment to "be with" them?

I have been blessed by "being with" my partner/team as . . .

(For example: *I have been blessed by "being with" my team as I have developed some special friendships that have enhanced my life and relationship with the Lord. Apart from anything we may have accomplished together, my life has been positively impacted because I know them as people who have accepted, encouraged, and loved me.*)

I sense that our team has been blessed by my priority of "being with" them as . . .

(For example: *I sense that our team has been blessed by my priority of "being with" them as we have had fewer conflicts and disagreements than ever before. I believe that is due to the fact that we have learned to truly care for one another before we start trying to "do things" together.*)

Share your responses with your partner or team as directed by your facilitator.

Transitions of Ministry: "Going Before the Lord" on Behalf of Your Team

Relational leaders must make the transition from "being with" people in ministry to "going before the Lord" on behalf of their team. As relational leaders develop caring and connected relationships with their team, the leader's role will occasionally need to change. Christ consistently modeled this principle as He turned aside to be in prayer with the Father. No doubt He often focused upon the eternal destiny of His calling, as well as interceding on behalf of His disciples.

Again, the story of Moses gives us insight into this transition. The seventeenth chapter of Exodus depicts the Israelites murmuring against Moses because they had no water to drink. Moses was faced with the challenge of internal complaints and realized that his ministry role needed to change. Scripture tells us how Moses addressed these challenges and reveals the necessity of our similar response. Moses cried out to the Lord, "What shall I do with these people?" and the Lord directed Moses to "go . . . before the people" (Exodus 17:4, 5 NKJV).

There will be times when you may discern that the people need a fresh sense of direction, a new vision or corporate goal. You may encounter challenges that have never occurred before. You may face new enemies, obstacles, or attacks you are unsure how to overcome. You, like Moses, may even face internal opposition or pervasive apathy. It will be at these times when God will move you toward a new role in ministry. Making such a transition will require significant personal growth. You will have to first "go before the Lord" to gain a sense of His direction, then "go before the people."

Relational leaders must be aware that fulfilling this new role of ministry will involve challenges to our ability to grow and adapt. First, there will be some who are so "with" people that their hearts are easily turned toward seeking man's approval. As leaders committed to personal growth, we must be willing to "go before" our team, secure in the approval that comes only from the Father. Only when we have a strong sense of His approval will we gain enough confidence and security to cast a vision for others. Seeking the Lord, regardless of others' approval, will also remind us that our strength and empowerment to accomplish ministry comes from Him. It is because of His provision that we can accomplish the vision and because of His blessings that we have the opportunity for ministry.

Second, our growth will be challenged as we make this transition because "going before the Lord" on behalf of the people helps us to recognize who it is we are really serving. When we are faced with the need to "go before the Lord" and seek His guidance on our team's behalf, we are reminded that it is His team, His vision, and His ministry. Beseeching the Lord helps us to remember the importance of listening to His voice and being able to sense His desires. As believers in Christ, we are to walk by faith, not by sight.

Personal Exercise #3

Reflect on your own experience of "going before the Lord." Do you remember times in the past when you found it important to seek the Lord? When have you encountered the challenges of ministry and been blessed because you went before the Lord on behalf of the people?

Did you seek the Lord because you . . .

- encountered new challenges or obstacles?
- encountered new enemies or attacks?
- faced ministry expansion or redirection?
- were faced with internal complaints, opposition, or apathy?

I remember "going before the Lord" when . . . and I can recall the importance of that because God . . .

You may also want to declare your recommitment and resolve to be more intentional about "going before the Lord" with future concerns.

I want to be more intentional about "going before the Lord" in the matters of . . .

Share your responses with your partner or small group as directed by your leader.

Transitions of Ministry: Entrusting Ministry to Others

One final area of growth that is necessary for the relational leader involves the transition of entrusting ministry to other people. After leaders have successfully developed a caring and connected team and begun to fulfill the vision God has ordained, many will be faced with the challenge and opportunity of expanding their vision. Leaders will ultimately conclude that in order to grow God's ministry, they must be willing to let go of certain areas of responsibility and allow other team members to step into those roles.

Once again we see this demonstration of growth and successful ministry transition in the life of Christ and the leadership of Moses. From the outset of His ministry, Christ prepared to entrust the "keys to the Kingdom" to His disciples. His plan involved both knowing and caring for them, as well as training and sending them out. He allowed them freedom to fail and encouraged them to press on. After Pentecost, His disciples turned the world upside down for Christ (Acts 2:41).

In Exodus 17:8–16, Moses entrusted the ministry to Joshua as they fought the battle against the Amalekites. The people might have grumbled about the change in leadership, and Moses himself might have felt more adequate fighting the battle than in this transitional role. But if Moses had resisted God's fresh calling, Israel would have been defeated. Scripture does not indicate that the multitudes had even been given a reason for the change in leadership. They did not know why Joshua led them into battle instead of Moses. But apparently, Moses had "been with" them in such a way that Israel trusted His wisdom in sending them into battle under Joshua's leadership.

Later, Moses faced the impossible task of trying to single-handedly provide for the needs of the children of Israel and settle the disputes among the hundreds of thousands of people who traveled together through the desert. Moses' father-in-law, Jethro, encouraged him to entrust some of the responsibilities of ministry to others. "The work is too heavy for you; you cannot handle it alone. . . . You must be the people's representative before God and bring their disputes to him. . . . But select capable men from all the people—men who fear God, trustworthy men who hate dishonest gain—and appoint them as officials over thousands, hundreds, fifties and tens. Have them serve as judges for the people at all times, but have them bring every difficult case to you; the simple cases they can decide themselves. That will make your load lighter, because they will share it with you" (see Exodus 18:13–27). God, through Jethro, challenged Moses to allow others to be a part of his expanding ministry, and as a result, Moses grew in his ability to shepherd the people.

Relational leaders realize that entrusting ministry to others is a vital part of growing themselves and growing the members of their team. Yet just as with the other transitions, the opportunities for growth will bring inevitable challenges. Team members may resist the change in leaders' roles, wanting to maintain the security and familiarity of times past. They may even complain that leaders are not as available, or that their new responsibilities are too difficult. But God wants the relational leader to face these transitions with confidence in His plan. By allowing others to take on new roles and responsibilities within the ministry, leaders will have more opportunities for personal growth, and the risk of stagnation within the ministry will decrease. God may also want to develop more faith in the heart of the leader as he or she is challenged to leave the familiar and potentially face personal insecurities and inadequacies.

God may want to develop more humility and trust within the heart of the leader as he or she faces the questions, "What if these others don't do as good a job as I could do? What will happen if they do a better job than I did? What if they receive more appreciation or more approval?" Finally, the Lord may want to cultivate a new confidence of God's ability in the leader, challenging him or her to trust God with fulfilling the vision and to leave the "designation of players" up to Him.

Personal Exercise #4

Consider your own tendency to entrust ministry to others. Take a few moments and reflect on this question.

As you think about transitioning into the role of "entrusting others with ministry," which of the following challenges might be most difficult for you?

- The complaints or grumblings of your team.
- The temptation to go back to the familiar rather than face your own inadequacies.
- The concern that others may not do a good job with their new role in the ministry.
- The concern that others may do a better job with their new role in the ministry.
- The concern that others may receive more appreciation or approval than you received.

As I think about my tendency to "entrust others with ministry," the most difficult part of that for me will be . . .

Share your responses with your team or small group as directed by your facilitator.

A critical principle that each relational leader must come to understand is the cyclical nature of these roles and transitions. A leader will first prioritize "being with" his or her team, and then as needed will move into the role of "going before the people." He or she will seek God for guidance, direction, and vision, and then lead the team toward the desires of the Lord. Next, the relational leader will be challenged by the necessity to entrust others with ministry as vision is expanded and ministry growth occurs. The wise leader understands, however, that this process is cyclical rather than linear. For example, a leader may be called upon to "be with" their team during particularly difficult situations or new struggles even if others have already been entrusted with ministry. At times, leaders need to come alongside and serve the team by "being with" them, thus communicating that they are not "too good" to yield to others' leadership. Other leaders will be faced with the challenge of needing to "be with" their team again after others' leadership has faltered or even failed. And at all stages of this process, leaders will need to be sensitive and available to times of "going before the Lord" on behalf of the people. Relational leaders recognize the dynamic nature of leading people, and come to accept the "few steps forward and few steps backward" that always seem to occur.

Personal Exercise #5

As a final step, take a few moments and assess your personal growth in each of the roles of ministry. Ask yourself the following questions and then share your responses:

What transitions are you currently being challenged to make in your own role within your team or ministry?

In my own role as a leader, I need to . . .

- "be with" my team members or others in the areas of . . .

- "go before the Lord" on behalf of my team members concerning . . .

- entrust ministry to other team members, such as . . .

I would like to address these transitions by . . .

Share your responses with your partner or small group as directed by your facilitator.

As you have assessed your personal growth in each of the roles of ministry, you have taken the first step toward continued growth. Being faithfully attentive to our own growth helps develop leadership traits such as personal responsibility, dependability, integrity, and the ability to balance competing life demands. But relational leaders are not only interested in personal growth. They are also committed to addressing the growth of others.

RELATIONAL LEADERS DEMONSTRATE COMMITMENT TO THE GROWTH OF OTHERS.

Throughout this course, we have challenged you in numerous areas of personal growth because relational leaders must first give an account to God for their own lives before they are prepared to lead others. We will now turn our attention to the leader's commitment to help others grow. If we are going to build a team that reaches its full potential as it fulfills the vision God has ordained, we must learn to develop other leaders and help them to grow.

Leading Others Through Transitions

As relational leaders encourage growth in others, it is important to follow a consistent process for addressing the transitions in others' roles. Leaders should see that their team members are equipped to do tasks, manage tasks, shepherd others, and eventually equip others for the work of the ministry. We will now focus upon Christ's example of "growing the disciples" and the intentional way in which He developed the future leaders of the church.

Encouraging team members to "do tasks." Relational leaders first demonstrate their commitment to the growth of others by giving team members the opportunity to perform certain jobs or accomplish specific tasks. In the early stages of Jesus' ministry with the disciples, many of them were only given one job: catching fish. Christ did not call the twelve and immediately ask them to begin preaching the Gospel or encourage them to lead anyone. He allowed them to perform simple tasks.

Likewise, as we strive to build a caring and connected team, we must first give team members the opportunity to carry out certain duties. Before we ask others to lead Bible studies or to oversee other facets of the ministry, we must first assess whether each person is comfortable doing simple jobs. Is this person able to help with the tasks of the ministry, tasks for which they may not receive recognition or praise? Is this person willing to assist with the less noticeable aspects of the ministry, or is he or she only interested in those tasks that are deemed "important"? Does this person have a humble heart? Does this person demonstrate a servant's spirit? As relational leaders who are committed to the growth of others, we must ask ourselves these questions about the members of our team, realizing that unless members demonstrate the humility necessary to "do tasks," they are not ready to lead or shepherd others. Furthermore, "doing tasks" helps develop and refine the enthusiasm of our team members. It is an enthusiastic team member who works heartily unto the Lord.

Encouraging team members to "manage tasks." As we build our team and continue our commitment to grow others, we must look for ways to increase team members' responsibility. After a team member has demonstrated the ability to "do tasks," they are then ready to "manage tasks." Relational leaders look for ways in which team members can further develop a servant's heart by giving them opportunities to help with administrative tasks, facilitate procedures, or direct existing programs.

As Jesus began to develop the disciples' leadership skills, He gave them opportunities to manage certain tasks within the ministry. For example, He asked the disciples to manage the task of grouping people and distributing loaves and fish during the feeding of the multitudes (Mark 6:39–44). Christ had sensed the disciples' humility and willingness to do simple tasks, and He was now giving them the opportunity to increase their responsibilities and to demonstrate leadership in small ways by managing the more administrative tasks of His ministry. From this example in the Gospels, we notice the intersection of doing tasks and interacting with people that comes with managing tasks. The disciples' task was simply to organize people in order to distribute food in an orderly manner. They may not have been ready to shepherd a person's soul, but as they interacted with people on the hills of Galilee, they developed kindness and respectful care along with a humble servant's heart. As we manage tasks and interact with people, God also works in **our** lives, helping to develop our respect for one another as we come to value and affirm the needs, ideas, and opinions of others.

Encouraging team members to shepherd others. As team members demonstrate their ability to do tasks and then manage tasks, the wise leader will look for ways to encourage these members to begin shepherding others. Many leaders stop too soon in their mentoring process, equipping others to manage certain aspects of the ministry but never challenging them to become shepherds themselves. We see Christ's challenge to the disciples in the Gospel of Matthew. Jesus sent the disciples out to preach, to heal, and to cast out demons because He was moved with compassion for those who were downcast and distressed, like a sheep without a shepherd (Matthew 9:36; 10:1). Relational leaders must issue this same challenge. We must look for those team members who are ready to begin sharing their life with others, thus becoming a shepherd to them and impacting their lives. At this point, all believers are challenged to coach, mentor, or disciple others as they pass on to them not only the gospel but their very lives (1 Thessalonians 2:7, 8). As other faithful men and women are raised up, the leadership trait of resourcefulness is developed. People's diverse talents, gifts, and callings are enlisted in caring connection with the team.

Encouraging team members to equip other shepherds. A final step in our commitment to grow others involves challenging our team members to begin equipping others in the same way that they have been equipped. The disciples became equippers of other shepherds in the 1st century church, radically changing the world for Christ and spreading the Gospel to an unbelieving world.

Equipping shepherds who can faithfully lead others requires great wisdom and judgment. In order to effectively equip others to lead, team members must possess the divine wisdom to discern the mind and heart of God, patiently waiting on His initiative in the midst of challenging possibilities, trusting His work in the life of others, and maintaining confidence that He who began a good work will be faithful to complete it (Philippians 1:6).

Being Relationally Involved in the Growth of Others

As we have discussed these important ministry transitions and the changing roles that leaders must successfully manage, some of you may be asking the question, "Where do I start? How do I inspire my team in these areas of growth?" Relational leaders encourage others to address these transitions through relational investing, relational encouragement, and relational intervention—the order of these steps being quite significant.

Relational investing involves focusing on those we lead, providing time, sensitivity, care, and attention just because we love them. Relational investing means giving to our team in these loving ways, all of which must be separated from our ministry's vision or a team member's performance. This expression of caring involvement helps bring freedom to others as they grow through transitions and continues to help team members separate who they are from what they do. Wise leaders often make these caring investments before particularly challenging or stressful events.

Relational encouragement involves encouraging others and building one another up, particularly when people seem "weary in well-doing" or when ministry seems stagnant (1 Thessalonians 5:11). Testimonies of God's blessings and the affirmation and appreciation of God's saints are vital parts of encouraging the team. The wise leader avoids issuing threats, making comparisons, displaying panic, or conveying condemnation or guilt in order to motivate or bring change. It is only love that "constrains" (2 Corinthians 5:14 KJV).

Relational intervention involves courageous love that sometimes reproves, corrects, or exhorts. Relational leaders will at times be required to "speak the truth in love" because they care for their team. Relational intervention may sound like, "I am burdened for you because . . ." or "I am concerned for you as I see. . . ." Intervention may also involve a leader's vulnerability— "It would mean a lot to me if you would . . ." or "I need your support in. . . ." At other times, intervention means doing nothing, allowing natural consequences to run their course, not interfering, or protecting someone from the consequences of their own actions.

Personal Exercise #6

Consider your commitment to build other leaders and stimulate growth among your team. Take a few moments and reflect on any ways you might increase your efforts in growing others.

What "growth transitions" might need to occur in others' roles within the team or ministry?

_____ needs to grow into _____.
Name   (managing/shepherding/equipping)

_____ needs to grow into _____.
Name   (managing/shepherding/equipping)

_____ needs to grow into _____.
Name   (managing/shepherding/equipping)

_____ needs to grow into _____.
Name   (managing/shepherding/equipping)

How might you be able to encourage these transitions?

I plan to encourage _____ by . . .

I plan to encourage _____ by . . .

I plan to encourage _____ by . . .

I plan to encourage _____ by . . .

Personal Exercise #7

You may also want to give specific attention to entrusting ministry to others and the issue of equipping in your own life. For instance, who are you presently training or equipping to do what you are now doing? How are you equipping other shepherds so that the work of the Lord is multiplied?

I am presently training _____ in the areas of . . .

I am presently training _____ in the areas of . . .

It would be important for me to entrust ministry to _____
in the areas of . . .

It would be important for me to entrust ministry to _____
in the areas of . . .

RELATIONAL LEADERS DEMONSTRATE COMMITMENT TO THE GROWTH OF THE MINISTRY.

Relational leaders must not only be committed to their own personal growth and the growth of the members of their team; they must also give priority to the growth of the ministry or church as a whole. It is vital that the leader have a sense of direction or a systematic process for pursuing that growth. As we conclude our discussion of relational leadership, we will summarize the conceptual process for building an effective team that is ready to implement any vision God places on your hearts.

Our Ministry Will Grow As We Care For One Another.

In our discussion of the priorities of the relational leader, we highlighted the importance of first "being with" your team before sending them out to do tasks. We also emphasized the importance of building a caring and connected team by learning how to meet one another's relational needs, thereby equipping your team to love like Christ. Likewise, the first step in ensuring ministry growth is learning to care for one another. That means being attentive, asking about each member's day, and truly stopping to listen. It involves learning about each other's "world" and entering into that world. It requires us to express comfort and care when someone is hurting. Wise leaders make it a priority to know if a team member is going through personal struggles or difficulties and to express compassionate care. A relational leader should never be too busy with "ministry vision" to hear about personal issues or too preoccupied with "ministry goals" to find time for individual concerns. Genuine care involves hurting with someone as they hurt, sharing words of comfort, and demonstrating compassion on that person's behalf.

Our Ministry Will Grow As We Trust One Another.

Growing a ministry requires that we truly know our team and let our team know us, which means that we must develop trust among one another. Trust is established as we mutually, vulnerably share our lives together, building upon the foundation of care we have already laid. Wise leaders learn to be vulnerable with their team, knowing that trust cannot be built if a leader hides behind position, status, or piety. Trust is enhanced as we learn to accept one another just as Christ has accepted us. Ministries grow as their members learn to look beyond people's faults and see their relational needs. As leaders model this acceptance and then encourage others in this way, they create an environment of safety, a place where people can be "real" with one another and still be loved. Personal hurts are shared because members feel safe. Even struggles with temptation are revealed because members know that they are free to share the imperfections of their lives and that they will be loved in spite of them. A strong sense of trust must be achieved in order for our ministries to truly flourish.

Our Ministry Will Grow As We Support One Another.

As we continue to pursue God's will for our ministry, we must support one another. Support will only come after a foundation of care and trust has been established. The wise relational leader refrains from announcing vision and then hoping that others will readily follow. The effective leader knows that once members come to sense that he or she truly cares about the team and can be trusted to demonstrate Christ's acceptance, their support will soon follow. As care is demonstrated, trust is built, and support of one another is established, the vision that may have begun within the mind and heart of the leader now becomes "our vision" instead of only "my vision." When a team truly cares for, trusts, and supports one another, and is collectively committed to a common goal, the ingredients for ministry growth and success are in place.

Our Ministry Will Grow As We Love One Another.

The final step in growing a ministry will naturally flow from the experience of care, trust, and support. As members of a team experience these three things, an environment of mutual love is created. This deep, mutual love then becomes contagious. Others will be drawn to our ministry and our churches as we demonstrate true, Christlike love for one another. The wise relational leader works intentionally to cultivate care, trust, and support, which will ultimately produce love. It will be our love that lets others know that we are Christ's disciples. Our ministry will grow as others see the love we have for one other. With our lives and our ministry, we will boldly declare the source of our love: "The God who is love!"

Personal Exercise #8

Take the next few moments and spend some time reflecting on how you sense that the Lord has impacted you during this study. How might He want you to change or grow? How might you go about making those changes?

In order to continue to grow as a relational leader, I want to especially keep in mind and heart . . .

I especially want to improve in my practice of . . .

Specifically, I plan to . . .

Close your time of reflection with a prayer of commitment to the Lord. Your prayer might sound like the following:

Lord, I am committed to grow in these ways as You enable me. May progress in these ways occur so that I, my family, and my ministry team might all be a part of your restoration of an identity of love to Your church! In Jesus' Name, Amen.

Share your responses with your partner or small group as directed by your facilitator. As everyone is comfortable, spend the last few moments praying aloud—in pairs or as a small group.

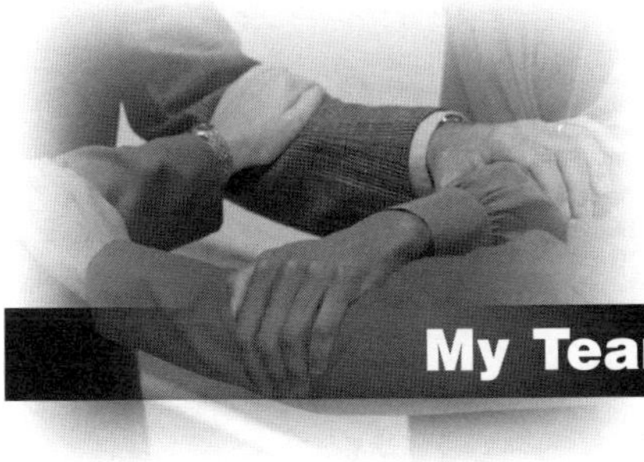

My Team Journal

■ How does each person in your team plan to continue their growth as a relational leader? What are their specific plans for accomplishing these goals?

Name: Responses:

_____

_____

_____

_____

_____

_____

Chapter 8 Outline

I. Characteristics of Meaningful Growth
   A. Meaningful Growth Will Be Sacrificial.

   Personal Exercise #1

   B. Meaningful Growth Will Be Mutual.

   Experiencing the Word Together

   C. Meaningful Growth Will Be Empowered by Gratitude.

II. Relational Leaders Demonstrate Commitment to Personal Growth.
   A. Transitions of Ministry: "Being With" Your Team

   Personal Exercise #2

   B. Transitions of Ministry: "Going Before the Lord" on Behalf of Your Team

   Personal Exercise #3

   C. Transitions of Ministry: Entrusting Ministry to Others

   Personal Exercise #4

   Personal Exercise #5

III. Relational Leaders Demonstrate Commitment to the Growth of Others.
   A. Leading Others Through Transitions
      1. From doing to managing
      2. From managing to shepherding
      3. From shepherding to equipping shepherds
   B. Being Relationally Involved in the Growth of Others
      1. Relational investing

    2. Relational encouragement

    3. Relational intervention

    Personal Exercise #6

    Personal Exercise #7

IV. Relational Leaders Demonstrate Commitment to the Growth of the Ministry.

  A. Our Ministry Will Grow as We Care for One Another.

  B. Our Ministry Will Grow as We Trust One Another.

  C. Our Ministry Will Grow as We Support One Another.

  D. Our Ministry Will Grow as We Love One Another.

    Personal Exercise #8

    My Team Journal

Additional Resources

Gareth Weldon Icenogle, _Biblical Foundations for Small Group Ministry_ (Downers Grove, IL: InterVarsity Press, 1994).

Stephen A. Macchia, _Becoming a Healthy Church_ (Grand Rapids, MI: Baker Books, 1999).

Alister McGrath, _Evangelicalism and the Future of Christianity_ (Downers Grove, IL: InterVarsity Press, 1995).

John R. W. Stott, _Evangelical Truth_ (Downers Grove, IL: InterVarsity Press, 1999).

NOTES

NOTES

About the Author

David Ferguson, along with his wife, Teresa, has shared a Biblical message of health and relevance for more than twenty-five years. Their passion for seeing the Great Commandment of loving God and loving others lived out among God's people has enabled them to impact thousands of ministers and their laity. As co-directors of Intimate Life Ministries, they direct a multi-disciplinary team which serves more than 35,000 churches in the United States and abroad with training and resources through the strategic partners involved in the Great Commandment Network of denominations, movements, and ministries. David serves as co-director of the Center for Relational Leadership, which provides training and resources in church, business, and community settings.

What is Intimate Life Ministries?

Intimate Life Ministries (ILM) is a training and resource ministry whose purpose is to assist in the development of on-going Great Commandment ministries worldwide. Great Commandment ministries help us love God and our neighbors through deepening our intimacy with God and with others in marriage, family, church, and community relationships.

Intimate Life exists to serve *The Great Commandment Network* of churches, ministries, and Christian leaders. This Network includes pastors and other ministry leaders, churches, para-church ministries and denominational partners representing over 35,000 churches in the U.S. and many others worldwide.

To serve the Great Commandment Network, ILM has developed a team consisting of:
- *Accredited Community Trainers* committed to helping churches establish ongoing Great Commandment ministries;
- *Professional Associates* from ministry and other professional Christian backgrounds, assisting with research, training, and resource development;
- *Christian broadcasters, publishers, media, and other affiliates,* cooperating to see Great Commandment ministries multiplied;
- *Headquarters staff* providing strategic planning, coordination, and support.

How Intimate Life Ministries Serves the Great Commandment Network (How Can We Serve You?)

1. *Ministering to Ministry Leaders*

- *Galatians 6:6 Retreats for Ministry Leaders* ILM offers a unique two-day *"Galatians 6:6" retreat* to ministers and their spouses for personal renewal and for reestablishing and affirming ministry and family priorities. The retreat accommodations and meals are provided as a gift to ministry leaders by co-sponsoring partners. Thirty to forty retreats are held throughout the U.S. and Europe each year.

- *Great Commandment Ministry On-line* provides tools and helps for pastors and ministry leaders including helpful downloads such as experiential sermons not available on the main pages of GreatCommandment.net, relational ministry team-building strategies, unique small group and Sunday School tools, and counseling tips from "Since You Asked." There are also tools to build your ministry teams through goal setting, assessing life balance, and time management.

- *Sermon Series* on Great Commandment topics to help pastors communicate a vision for Great Commandment health as well as identify and cultivate a core lay leadership group.

2. *Partnerships with Denominations and Other Ministries Offering Tools to Support Relational Ministry Vision*

- *Partnerships with Denominations and Other Ministries* Various denominations and ministries have partnered with ILM to equip their ministry leaders through the *Galatians 6:6* Retreats, along with strategic training and experiential resources for ongoing ministry. These partnerships enable partner organizations to use the expertise of ILM trainers and resources to perpetuate a movement of Great Commandment ministry at the local level. ILM also provides a crisis-support setting where partners may send ministers, couples, or families who are struggling in their relationships.

3. *Identifying, Training, and Equipping Relational Leaders*
ILM is committed to helping the church develop relational leaders through:

- Experiential, user-friendly *curriculum materials* for deepening Great Commandment love. All courses are video-assisted and complete with detailed workbooks and leaders' guides.

- *Weekend Workshops* for enriching relationships and implementing Great Commandment ministry in the local church through marriage, parenting, or single adult workshops. Conducted by Intimate Life Community Trainers, these workshops are a great way to jump-start Great Commandment ministry within the local church.

- **Great Commandment Life On-Line** Provides tools for relationships and the workplace including helpful downloads such as family night tips, marriage staff meeting ideas, daily couples devotionals, and ways singles can reach out to other single adults by meeting relational needs. Tools for the workplace include goal setting, time management, and life balance assessment.

- **Great Commandment Living Conferences** for promoting church and ministry relevance in a postmodern world by helping us know and love God as He really is, experience God's Word, and know and love people with His love.

- **Relational Ministry Leader Accreditation program** An on-line supported, structured process for guiding church leaders through relational ministry training. This program is for those who wish to be better equipped to lead relational ministry in their local churches and communities.

4. *Providing Crisis Support and Counselor / Caregiver Training*

The ILM Center for Relational Care (CRC) provides therapy and support to relationships in crisis through an accelerated process of growth and healing, including the Relational Care Intensives™ for couples, families, and singles. The CRC also offers training for counselors and caregivers through *More Than Counseling* seminars.

For more information on how you, your church, ministry, denomination, or movement can become part of the Great Commandment Network and take advantage of the services and resources offered by Intimate Life Ministries, write or call:

Intimate Life Ministries
P.O. Box 201808
Austin, TX 78720-1808
800-881-8008

Or visit our website:
www.GreatCommandment.net